Hearing with the Eye

Hearing with the Eye

Photographs from Point Lobos

with commentary on Master Dogen's "Teachings of the Insentient"

John Daido Loori

Published by
Dharma Communications

For information, write Dharma Communications at
P.O. Box 156, South Plank Road, Mt. Tremper, NY 12457

9   8   7   6   5   4   3   2   1

First Edition
Printed in China

Library of Congress Number: 2004107250

ISBN 1-882795-19-9

Contents

*This book is dedicated to the insentient
and their wondrous expression of the Way.*

Acknowledgments

First and foremost, I must express my gratitude to Eihei Dogen, whose rich poetic imagery and profound teachings inspired and guided the creation of my visual and prose commentary.

I am grateful to Konrad Ryushin Marchaj and Vanessa Zuisei Goddard of Dharma Communications Press for their council and skillful editing of the manuscript, to Chris Koto Trevelyan for his graphics and layout work, and to Andrew Hobai Pekarik for his translation of Dogen's original text.

I also wish to acknowledge the many participants in the intensive "Teachings of the Insentient" workshop offered at Zen Mountain Monastery. Their questions and comments helped to shape the language of this book, making Dogen's teachings more accessible to the western reader.

How extraordinary! How extraordinary!
The insentient express the Way! How mysterious!
If you listen with the ears, it is incomprehensible.
If you hear sounds with the eyes, it is truly knowable.

— Zen Master Dongshan

1. Expressing the Way through the Way that expresses is the actualization of the teaching that "realized ones transmit the lineage to realized ones." Expressing the Way is the same as the Way expressing. It is not sentient. It is not insentient. It is not intentional. It is not unintentional. It is not caused by either the intentional or the unintentional. It is not caused by conditions. Nonetheless, although, like the flight of birds, it leaves no traces, it is intentionally provided to the assembly of realized ones. When the Great Way fully comes into being, expressing the Way fully comes into being. When the treasury of the Way is transmitted, expressing the Way is transmitted. When the flower of realization is raised, expressing the Way is raised. When the robe is transmitted, expressing the Way is transmitted. For this reason, all the realized ones, in the same way, from the beginning of time, have humbly attended to expressing the Way. All realized ones, from the beginning, have taken expressing the Way as their fundamental practice. Do not study this with the idea that expressions of the Way are only something that realized ones end up creating. Realized ones end up being created by the expressing of the Way.

2. This expressing the Way is not just the opening of the nearly 84,000 gates of the Way, it is the expressing of the Way that has infinite, limitless gates. Do not study with the idea that today's realized ones express the expressions of the earlier realized ones. Just as the realized ones of the past do not reappear and become today's realized ones, so too yesterday's expressing of the Way should not be taken as today's. For that reason, Shakyamuni said, "In the same way that the realized ones of the three existences expressed the Way, I, too, will now express a Way that is without distinctions." Therefore, just as we use the expressions of all realized ones, all realized ones use the expressing of the Way. Just as the expressions of all realized ones are correctly transmitted, all realized ones correctly transmit the expressing of the Way. Accordingly, there is the insentient expressing of the Way, correctly transmitting from the ancient realized ones to the Past Seven Buddhas and from the Past Seven Buddhas to the present. All realized ones and all their ancestors exist within this insentient expressing of the Way. As for my present expressing of the Way, do not study it as if it were a new branch separate from the true transmission. As for the true transmission from the past, do not realize it as if it were an ancient nest or a demon's cave.

3. Once a monastic asked the Tang Dynasty Chinese National Teacher, Nanyang, "Do the insentient understand the expressing of the Way?" The National Teacher said, "They express the Way continually, energetically, ceaselessly." The monastic said, "Why can't I hear it?" The National Teacher replied, "The fact that you don't hear it has nothing to do with others hearing it." The monastic said, "I don't understand. What kind of person can hear it?" The National Teacher said, "All the holy ones can hear it." The monastic asked, "Do you hear it?" The National Teacher said, "I do not hear it." The monastic said, "If you do not hear it, how do you know that the insentient can express the Way?" The National Teacher said, "Fortunately I do not hear it. If I did, I would be one of the holy ones and you would not be able to hear me expressing the Way." The monastic said, "In that case, sentient

beings can't hear it." The National Teacher said, "I express the Way for the sake of sentient beings, not for the sake of the holy ones." The monastic said, "Then what happens when sentient beings do hear you?" The National Teacher said, "At that moment they are not sentient beings."

4. Whether they are beginners or advanced practitioners, those who wish to study the insentient expressing the Way should carefully study the teaching of this National Teacher. He said, "They express the Way continually, energetically, ceaselessly. " "Continually" is the single moment within all time. Regarding the words "expressing ceaselessly," in the same way that "expressing" is already manifest, it necessarily is "ceaseless." Do not study this with the thought that the insentient expressing of the Way is just like the sentient. The realized Way does not fake the sounds of the insentient world by stealing the voices and sounds of the sentient world so that they resemble the sentient expressing the Way. The insentient expressing of the Way is not at all a physical sound heard with the ears, in the same way that the sentient expressing of the way is not a physical sound either.

5. You should study diligently, asking yourself and asking others, "What is sentient? What is insentient?" You should study precisely and with all your heart the question of what is the meaning of the phrase "the insentient express the Way." The foolish conclude that the sound of branches in the forest or the opening of flowers and the falling of leaves are the insentient expressing the Way. They are not people who have studied the realized Way. If it were so, who would not know the insentient expressing the Way? Who would not hear the insentient expressing the Way? You should take time to turn a light on this. In the world of the insentient are there grasses, trees, and forests, or not? Is the world of the insentient blended in with the world of the sentient, or not? However, if you consider grasses, trees, tiles, and stones, and take them to be the insentient, this is limited knowledge. If you consider the concept "insentient," and take it to be grasses, trees, tiles, and stones, you have not arrived at fullness.

6. Even if we were to take the grasses, trees, and so forth that people see and regard them as insentient, grasses and trees are not matters for ordinary thinking to determine. Consider some of the reasons. Forests in the world of heavenly beings are clearly special, and not at all the same as the forests of China and its environs. Grasses and trees of the sea are different from the grasses and trees of the mountains. Moreover, the sky has forests, clouds have forests, and hundreds of grasses and thousands of trees are born and mature amid fire and wind. In general there are those that have been studied as sentient; there are those that have not been taken as insentient. Some grasses and trees are human-like or animal-like. The sentient and insentient are not yet clarified. When it comes to the trees, rocks, flowers, fruits and water of the hermits, for example, even when they do not doubt what they see, it is hard for them to explain it in words. Don't conclude with a categorization that says that because you saw some of the grasses and trees of China, and because you are familiar with the grasses and trees of Japan, the inexhaustible worlds in all directions must be like this too.

7. The National Teacher said, "All the holy ones can hear it." He said that among the disciples of the insentient expressing the Way, all the holy ones stand on the ground and listen. The holy ones and the insentient together actualize hearing, and bring about the actualization of expressing. The insentient express the Way for the sake of all holy ones. Are the insentient holy? Are they ordinary? Those who have finally clarified the meaning of the insentient expressing the Way fully embody that which is heard by all the holy ones. Once you attain this embodiment, you will know how to identify the realm of the holy ones. Moreover, you should study thoroughly the walk along the night path that transcends both the holy and the ordinary.

The National Teacher, Nanyang, said, "I do not hear it." Do not take this as something that is easy to understand. Does he not hear because he has surpassed the ordinary and gone beyond the holy? Does he not hear because he has broken open the ordinary and the holy, the nest and the cave? Make an effort in this way and you will actualize his teaching.

8. The National Teacher said, "Fortunately I do not hear it. If I did, I would be a holy one." What he is pointing to here is not just some words. "Fortunately I" is not ordinary or holy. Is "fortunately I" a realized one? Because the realized ones have surpassed the ordinary and gone beyond the holy, that which they hear is certainly not the same as what all holy ones hear.

By cultivating the logic of the National Teacher's words, "Then you would not hear me expressing the Way," you can practice the enlightened wisdom of all realized ones and all holy ones. The key point is that all holy ones can hear the insentient expressing the Way. We practitioners can hear the National Teacher expressing the Way. Make an effort to study this teaching throughout the days, throughout the months. You should take the time to ask the National Teacher, "I don't ask about the time after all beings hear, but what about the exact moment when all beings hear the expressing of the Way?"

Master Dongshan, when he was studying under Master Yunyan, asked him, "The insentient express the Way. What kind of person can hear it?" Yunyan replied, "The insentient express the Way, and the insentient can hear it." Dongshan asked, "Do you hear it, or not?" Yunyan replied, "If I heard it, you would not be able to hear me expressing the Way." Dongshan said, "If that's the case, then I do not hear you expressing the Way." Yunyan said, "I am expressing it and still you do not hear. How much less likely that you will hear the insentient expressing the Way." Dongshan composed this verse and offered it to Yunyan, saying:

How extraordinary! How extraordinary!
The insentient express the Way! How mysterious!
If you listen with the ears, it is incomprehensible.
If you hear sounds with the eyes, it is truly knowable.

9. Now, with regard to this teaching of Master Dongshan, "What kind of person can hear the insentient expressing the Way?" you should make a good and careful investigation through this life and many lives. This question also provides the virtue and benefit of a teaching. This teaching has skin, flesh, bones and marrow. It is not only the mind being transmitted by the mind. Mind being

transmitted by mind is the practice and affirmation of both beginners and advanced practitioners. There is a barrier key that is correctly transmitted by the offering of the robe, and that is correctly transmitted by the raising of the teaching. Present day people—how can they reach the ultimate in only three or four years of effort?

Though it is said that Dongshan had heard and seen the main point of Nanyang's earlier statement that "all holy ones can hear the insentient expressing the Way," there is now, additionally, his question—"What kind of person can hear the insentient expressing the Way?" Do you take this as affirming Nanyang's statement? Do you take it as denying Nanyang's statement? Do you take it as a question? Do you take it as a statement? If it completely denies Nanyang, how do you take Dongshan's words? If it completely affirms Nanyang, then how do you understand Dongshan's words?

10. Dongshan's teacher, Yunyan, said, "The insentient express the Way, and the insentient can hear it." Correctly transmitting this lineage, there is study by means of the dropping away of body and mind. This statement, "the insentient express the Way, and the insentient can hear it" is identical to "all realized ones express the Way and all realized ones are able to hear it." An assembly that would listen to the insentient expressing the Way, whether it is composed of sentient beings or insentient beings, whether it is made up of ordinary people or wise and holy ones, would be an assembly of the insentient. By means of this complete reality, one can distinguish truth from falsehood both in the past and in the present. Even if a teacher arrives from India, if he is not an authentic teacher of the true transmission, you should not follow him. Even if something was practiced continuously for one thousand or ten thousand years, if it was not mutually passed from heir to heir, it will be hard to carry on. Today the true transmission is well known in China and it should be easy to distinguish what is true and what is false. If you listen to the teaching, "All beings express the Way, and all beings can hear it," you will receive the bones and marrow of all the realized ones and all their ancestors.

11. If you hear the words of Yunyan and listen to the words of Nanyang, and truly take them in, you will know that "all the holy ones" in the statement "All the holy ones can hear," are insentient, and you will know that "the insentient" in the statement "the insentient can hear" are all holy ones. This is because that which the insentient express is insentient, and the insentient expressing the Way is itself insentient. In other words, the insentient express the Way, and the expressing of the Way is insentient.

Dongshan said, "If that's the case, then I do not hear you expressing the Way." This phrase, "If that's the case," highlights the main point of Yunyan's statement "The insentient express the Way, and the insentient can hear it." In accordance with the teaching that "The insentient express the Way, and the insentient can hear it," comes "I do not hear you expressing the Way." With these words Dongshan did not just touch the edge of the seat of the insentient expressing the Way, he struck the sky by making apparent his intentions towards the insentient expressing the Way. This is not just fully accomplishing the insentient expressing the Way, it is fully investigating both hearing and not hearing the insentient expressing the Way. Going further, he brought about the full accomplishment of expressing, not expressing, past expressing, present expressing, and future expressing of the sentient expressing the Way. Moreover, in the end he also clarified the teaching that hearing and not hearing the expressing of the Way are both sentient and insentient.

12. In general, hearing the teachings of the Way is not just a matter of physical hearing or conscious hearing. It is hearing the teachings with all force, all mind, all body, all speech, from as far in the past as before your father and mother were born, before the first sound in the universe, up to the limit of the future and the unlimited future beyond that. It is hearing the teachings before the body and after the mind. These ways of hearing the teachings always have benefits. Do not say that there is no benefit in hearing the teachings unless the hearing is conditioned by consciousness. Even those whose minds are not operating and whose bodies have collapsed can obtain benefit from hearing the teachings. Those without minds and without bodies can obtain benefit from hearing the teachings. All realized ones and all ancestors without fail spent time like this, and in so doing they created realized ones and became ancestors. How can ordinary thinking completely comprehend that the power of the teachings touches the body and the mind? Ordinary thinking is unable by itself to completely clarify the limits of body and mind.

13. Whenever the merit and virtue of hearing the teachings are planted in the field of the mind and body, they never wither. Hearing the teachings inevitably matures and bears fruit. Foolish people think that if they do not advance on the path of understanding and cannot remember the teachings even though they hear them constantly, then there is no merit. They think they must listen frequently to learning and writings with their whole mind and body. They think, "What benefit can there be if I forget the talk while still on my seat and feel uncertain as I get up? What educational merit could there be?" They think like this because they have not encountered, or even seen, an authentic teacher. An authentic teacher is someone who has received the authentic transmission face-to-face. An authentic teacher is someone to whom the realized ones have truly transmitted. When foolish people say they are conscious of some teachings and remember them for a short time, those are the times when the efficacy of hearing the teachings, even if they are only slightly aware of it, envelops the mind and envelops consciousness.

14. Exactly at authentic moments like these, there are the merits and virtues of enveloping the body, enveloping what is before the body, enveloping the mind, enveloping what is before the mind, enveloping what is after the mind, enveloping causes, results, actions, conditions, natures, forms, power, enveloping the Buddha, enveloping the ancestors, enveloping self and other, enveloping skin, flesh, bones, and marrow, and so forth. By actualizing the merits and virtues of enveloping words and expression and enveloping sitting and lying down, they reach everywhere, from the smallest waves to the sky.
   Truly it is hard to know the merit and virtue of this kind of hearing of the teachings. Nonetheless, if you meet in the great assembly of realized ones, and investigate the skin, flesh, bones, and marrow, you will ceaselessly draw the merit and power of the expressing of the

teachings and there will be no place that you do not envelop with the spiritual power of hearing the teachings. Practicing in this way, whether the waves of the eons are slow or fast, you will eventually see the actualization of results. Although we should not irrationally throw out frequently listening to learning and writings, neither should we take this single aspect as an essential point. Those who study know this. Dongshan embodied this fully.

15. Yunyan said, "I am expressing it and still you do not hear. How much less likely that you will hear the insentient expressing the Way." In response to this actualization of the enlightenment of Dongshan, which immediately went beyond enlightenment, verifying even the vow of enlightenment, Yunyan opened his heart to Dongshan, thus sealing and verifying the bones and marrow of the ancestors. "You still do not hear when I express it." His is not the everyday meaning of these words. He is verifying and clarifying that the insentient expressing the Way, even if it has ten thousand aspects, is not the object of thinking. The continuation of the lineage on this occasion is what is key. Neither ordinary people nor the holy ones can easily reach and inquire into this.

Dongshan then composed a verse and offered it to Yunyan, saying, "The mystery of the insentient expressing the Way is so extraordinary, so extraordinary!" Both the insentient and the insentient expressing the Way are hard to conceptualize. What sort of thing is this "insentient" that he speaks about? You should study how it is neither ordinary nor holy, sentient nor insentient. The ordinary, the holy, the sentient, the insentient, together with expressing and not expressing— all belong to the realm of the conceptual.

16. The insentient, right now, is mysterious and wondrous and yet again wondrous. It goes beyond the knowledge and consciousness of ordinary people and wise holy ones. It is not connected to the calculations of heavenly beings or humans.

"If you listen with the ears, it is incomprehensible." Even if you had heavenly ears, even if you had ears of the Way that span worlds and span time, when you try listening with the ears it is incomprehensible. Even if you had ears on top of a wall or ears on the head of a stick, you would not understand the insentient expressing the Way. That's because it is not a physical sound. It is not that there is no listening with the ears, but even if you exhausted 100,000 eons of effort, it would be incomprehensible. The insentient expressing the Way is a direct way of being, which is apart from sounds and forms; it is not a nest or cave in the realm of the ordinary or the holy.

"If you hear sounds with the eyes, it is truly knowable." Nowadays people think that hearing sounds with the eyes refers to the coming and going of grasses, trees, blossoms, or birds, which are seen with the eyes. This idea is mistaken, and is not at all the Buddha's teaching.

17. In studying Dongshan's "hear sounds with the eye," it is the eye where one hears the sound of the insentient expressing the Way. It is the eye where one manifests the sound of the insentient expressing the Way. You should study this eye extensively. Because the eye's hearing sound ought to be the same as the ear's hearing sound, the eye's hearing sound is *not* the same as the ear's hearing sound. Do not study with the idea that there is an ear faculty within the eye.

Do not study with the idea that the eye is identical to the ear. Do not study with the idea that sound is manifest behind the eye.

18. An ancient said, "All the worlds in the ten directions are a monastic's single eye." Do not compare these teachings and conclude that if one were to hear sounds with this single eye, it would be the same as Dongshan's teaching of "hearing sounds with the eyes." Even though we study the ancient's words, "all the worlds in the ten directions," and "a single eye," all ten directions *are* just this single eye. Moreover, there is the eye of a thousand hands. There is the eye of the true teachings. There is the eye of a thousand ears. There is the eye of a thousand tongues. There is the eye of a thousand minds. There is the eye of a thousand realized minds. There is the eye of a thousand realized bodies. There is the eye of a thousand staffs. There is the eye of a thousand precursors of the body. There is the eye of a thousand precursors of the mind. There is the eye of a thousand deaths in death. There is the eye of a thousand lives in life. There is the eye of a thousand selves. There is the eye of a thousand others. There is the eye of a thousand eyes. There is the eye of a thousand studies. There is the eye of a thousand verticals. There is the eye of a thousand horizontals.

19. Therefore, if you study all eyes as all worlds, still you do not investigate deeply into the eye. Just make an urgent effort to investigate, by means of your eye, hearing the insentient expressing the Way. Now, the point of Dongshan's teaching is that it is hard for the ear to understand the insentient expressing the Way. The eye hears sounds. Moreover, there is hearing sounds with the realized body. There is hearing sounds with the all-pervasive body. Even if you do not investigate the eye hearing sounds, you should physically attain "the insentient can hear the insentient express the Way." You should drop away body and mind.

20. Because this teaching was passed on, my late teacher Jujing, the old Buddha, said, "The gourd vine entangles the gourd." This is "expressing the Way," and the "insentient," through which the true eye of Dongshan has been passed on, through which the bones and marrow of Dongshan have been passed on. Due to the teaching that everything that expresses the Way is insentient, this is the insentient expressing the Way, and is what is called a "textual precedent." The insentient is that which expresses the Way for the sake of the insentient. What is it that is called "insentient"? You should know. It is that which listens to the insentient expressing the Way. What is it that is called "expressing the Way"? You should know. It is that which does not know that it is itself insentient.

A monastic once asked Great Master Touzi, "What is 'the insentient expressing the Way?'" The Master said, "Don't speak ill." Now, what Master Touzi teaches is surely the spiritual charter of the ancient realized ones, the governing edict of the lineage of ancestors. Both "the insentient express the Way" and "that which expresses the Way is insentient" are not speaking ill. You should know this. "The insentient expressing the Way" is the complete text of the realized ones and ancestors. The followers of Linji and Deshan do not know it. Only one-by-one do the realized ones and ancestors investigate it, realize it, and actualize it.

Introduction

Eihei Dogen, a thirteenth century Zen Buddhist master and founder of the Japanese school of Soto Zen Buddhism, is one of the most highly respected teachers in the history of Zen. Dogen has recently been discovered in the West, and is widely respected as a great religious thinker and outstanding writer and poet.

Dogen began his monastic studies at the Tiandai (J. Tendai) monastery on Mount Hiei in Kyoto. After training at several other monasteries, he then moved to Kenninji—also a Tiandai temple—in Kyoto. Here, the priest Eisai, having just returned from China, was introducing the teaching and practice methods of Chinese Zen that he had learned from teachers of the Linji school of Zen Buddhism. For the next seven years after Eisai's death, Dogen continued his studies under Eisai's successor, Myozen, and with him traveled to China. Once there, Dogen met Master Jujing and decided to stay and study with him. Attaining enlightenment under Jujing, Dogen received dharma transmission, then returned to Japan in the year 1227. He again took up residence at Kenninji, this time as a certified teacher in the Caodong (J. Soto) lineage—a Zen line that was unknown in Japan at the time. Indeed, much of what was then called "Zen" was a mix of Linji (J. Rinzai) Zen and Tiandai Buddhism. Dogen remained teaching in the Kyoto area for some fifteen years, then established Eiheiji temple in the remote mountains of Echizen.

Today we know of Dogen's teaching through the texts that have come down to us from those years spent at Kenninji and Eiheiji. Dogen's masterwork, the *Shobogenzo: Treasury of the True Dharma Eye*, consists of ninety-two extensive discourses on Zen Buddhism, and it represents more than half of his literary output. The remainder of his contributions to Zen literature consists of a number of works, among them *Fukanzazengi* (General Advice on the Principle of Zazen), *Zuimonki* (Master Dogen's Sayings), *Tenzokyokun* (Instructions to the Chief Cook), *Bendoho* (Rules for Practicing the Way), *Eiheikoroku* (A Record of Master Eihei's Sayings) and several works regarding monastic rules, as well as the organization and management of a monastery.

When Dogen settled down to teach at Kenninji, among the students who gathered there were members of the Daruma school of Buddhism. These monastics were trained in koan introspection, so in his teachings Dogen sprinkled koans drawn from three hundred classic cases he had collected during his travels in China. Today this volume is known as the *Mana* or *Chinese Shobogenzo*. Dogen used these koans as seeds for his writings and lectures. Several of them appear in "Mujo Seppo" (Teachings of the Insentient), the *Shobogenzo* chapter that forms the starting point of this book.

The concept of the insentient or inanimate expounding the Buddhist teachings first appeared in the Indian Buddhist scripture, the *Flower Garland Sutra*, written during the first century C.E. Centuries later, this sutra was translated into Chinese, and it became an important part of Chinese Buddhism, particularly in the Zen and Flower Garland (C. Huayan, J. Kegon) Schools.

The question of whether or not inanimate beings possessed buddha nature and were capable of expressing the teachings was at the center of many discussions in early Tang dynasty China, all of which were based on differing interpretations of the *Nirvana* and the *Flower Garland* sutras. As a result, many encounters between monastics and various masters of the time centered around the nature of the expression of these teachings.

In "Mujo Seppo," Master Dogen follows the progression of a set of such dialogues, beginning with an encounter between the Chinese Tang Dynasty National Teacher Nanyang (675-775, C.E.) and an unnamed monastic. The National teacher cites the *Flower Garland Sutra*, saying: "The earth expounds the teachings, living beings expound the teachings. Throughout the three times, everything expounds the teachings." Then a monastic named Dongshan (807-869, C.E.), who was later to become one of the greatest Zen masters—as well as the founder of the Caodong school—takes up the National Teacher's statement. First he visits Master Guishan (771-853, C.E.) looking for elaboration. Guishan briefly instructs Dongshan, but Dongshan doesn't understand him, so Guishan sends him to Master Yunyan (782-841, C.E.). In his dialogue with Master Yunyan, Dongshan finally experiences deep enlightenment and becomes Yunyan's successor.

Four centuries later, and in the same lineage, Master Dogen also deals with these teachings of the insentient. They first appear in 1240 in his work "Keiseisanshiki" (Sounds of the Valley Streams, Form of the Mountains); again, in the year 1240 in "Sansuikyo" (Mountains and Rivers Sutra); and finally, in 1243, after his move to Echizen province and shortly before the establishment of his new monastery Eiheiji, Dogen writes the present chapter.

Eight more centuries have passed, and we revisit this teaching here in the West. The translation presented in this work is based on a previous translation by Andrew Hobai Pekarik of the "Mujo Seppo" chapter of Dogen's *Shobogenzo,* as it appears in the edition annotated by Mizuno Yaoko (*Shobogenzo* published by Iwanami Shoten, Tokyo, 1991, vol. 3, pages 54-73). This translation was one of a few existing English translations of this same chapter used during a week-long intensive study at Zen Mountain Monastery. Through discussions and a thorough examination of Master Dogen's teachings, a new composite translation evolved that we feel still retains the spirit of the original, and at the same time, is more accessible to an English-speaking audience.

Nowadays, there are several commentaries that adequately address the work of Master Dogen. In this book, I have used both prose and poetry to elaborate on his profound teachings, as well as the added dimension of the visual image. It has always been my feeling that somewhere between the words that describe the reality, and the reality itself, exists a space that can be filled by the photograph. When such an image is perceived not just with the eye, but with the whole body and mind, then one understands "it" intimately.

We must keep in mind that to engage in this kind of study is not an easy matter, mainly because the kind of teaching contained within these pages is what we call in Buddhism "intimate expression." Although in intimate expression there is no sound, still, it cannot be called silent. This is not a matter that can be grasped by linear, sequential thought. It's not to be found in the realm of dualistic thinking. We must realize it in the realm of intimacy itself—where image, reader and word merge into a single reality.

John Daido Loori
Zen Mountain Monastery
Tremper Mountain, New York
Summer 2004

Expressing the Way through the Way that expresses is the actualization of the teaching that "realized ones transmit the lineage to realized ones." Expressing the Way is the same as the Way expressing. It is not sentient. It is not insentient. It is not intentional. It is not unintentional. It is not caused by either the intentional or the unintentional. It is not caused by conditions. Nonetheless, although, like the flight of birds, it leaves no traces, it is intentionally provided to the assembly of realized ones. When the Great Way fully comes into being, expressing the Way fully comes into being. When the treasury of the Way is transmitted, expressing the Way is transmitted. When the flower of realization is raised, expressing the Way is raised. When the robe is transmitted, expressing the Way is transmitted. For this reason, all the realized ones, in the same way, from the beginning of time, have humbly attended to expressing the Way. All realized ones, from the beginning, have taken expressing the Way as their fundamental practice. Do not study this with the idea that expressions of the Way are only something that realized ones end up creating. Realized ones end up being created by the expressing of the Way.

Commentary 1

The mountain form is the body of truth;
only the ear can see it.
The valley sounds are the voice of the teachings;
only the eye can hear them.

Expressing the Way through the Way that expresses is the actualization of the teaching that "realized ones transmit the lineage to realized ones." In other words, the act of expressing the Way is the realized truth of the universe transmitted from realized ones to realized ones. This process of transmission is "the Way expressing." Another way of saying this is that the teachings of the insentient are realized by sages and holy ones, as well as transmitted by sages and holy ones. What does it mean to realize the teachings of the insentient? And how is this realization transmitted to subsequent generations?

The teachings of the insentient have nothing to do with understanding, nor with believing. They require a kind of cognition—a realization—that does not come from the outside. Why? Because it is the inherent nature of all beings. It is the insentient realizing the insentient.

We must understand that in the Zen transmission of the Way, nothing moves from A to B. The teacher doesn't give anything to the student. The student already has what the teacher has. It just needs to be awakened. The function of the teacher is simply to provide the expedient means to facilitate the student's process of discovery.

Expressing the Way, "like the flight of birds, leaves no traces." That is, this expressing does not fall into a dualistic framework. The "track of birds" is a traceless track, because it is nondual. It can't be appreciated from a fixed perspective. It is not sentient and it's not insentient. It's not intentional and it's not unintentional. It does not follow cause and effect, and it's not outside of cause and effect. Therefore, expressing the Way does not move along the track of birds.

The apparently paradoxical expression of the Way in this chapter is characteristic of Dogen's teachings. Negating the extremes, he points to the inconceivable. It's not this side; it's not that side—it's the inconceivable. Dogen says in the "Mountains and Rivers Sutra," "The stone woman gives birth to a child in the night"—inconceivable. "The wooden man jumps up and dances"— inconceivable. Your life and my life— inconceivable. The fundamental nature of reality is inconceivable. This inconceivability is implicit in Buddhism, from the beginning of the first teachings through the entirety of spiritual training. It is constantly affirmed whenever two dualities come together as one reality. And it can only be appreciated when we understand the interpenetration, interdependence, and non-interference of all dualities. The truth is not form. It's not emptiness. It's not both. It's not neither. It is inconceivable. Yet, it exists thus.

In "Genjokoan: The Way of Everyday Life," another chapter from the *Shobogenzo*, Dogen states:

When all dharmas are buddhadharma, there's life and death, buddhas and creatures, practice, enlightenment and delusion. When the ten thousand things return to the self, there is no life, no death, no buddhas, no creatures, no enlightenment, no delusion.

The first statement is affirming. The second statement is negating. Then there is the third line:

However, the Buddha Way is beyond being and non-being; therefore, there is life, there is death, there are buddhas, there are creatures, there is enlightenment, there is delusion.

There is expounding the teachings. There is Dogen expounding the teachings. There is the inanimate revealing the truth of the universe.

In Zen there are various ways of teaching. All of them are a direct pointing to the human mind-heart. They are skillful means to help people verify for themselves their own true nature. There is meditation. There are discourses and talks, koans, face-to-face meetings with the teacher, records of the masters. But, Dogen emphasizes here, there are also the teachings offered by the insentient. Again, he says in the "Mountains and Rivers Sutra:" "These mountains and rivers of the present are a manifestation of the teachings of the ancient sages." There is the teaching of the flower held up by the Buddha on Mount Gridhrakuta. There is the teaching of the staff, the fly whisk, the meditation cushion. There is the teaching of the sounds of the valley streams and the form of the mountain. One master gained realization upon hearing a stone strike a bamboo stalk. Another had insight upon seeing plum blossoms. These are all examples of the insentient expressing the Way.

To receive the teachings we must be totally present to them. All of the ancestors, all practitioners, all the realized ones, from the beginning of time, have humbly attended to expressing the Way. Having openly attended to the expressing of the Way by the insentient, all realized ones have ended up being created by the expressing of the Way. But we should realize that this in no way makes them dependent upon the teachings of the insentient. Actually, it is the teachings of the insentient that rely on them.

When the Great Way fully comes into being,
expressing the Way fully comes into being.

This expressing the Way is not just the opening of the nearly 84,000 gates of the Way, it is the expressing of the Way that has infinite, limitless gates. Do not study with the idea that today's realized ones express the expressions of the earlier realized ones. Just as the realized ones of the past do not reappear and become today's realized ones, so too yesterday's expressing of the Way should not be taken as today's. For that reason, Shakyamuni said, "In the same way that the realized ones of the three existences expressed the Way, I, too, will now express a Way that is without distinctions." Therefore, just as we use the expressions of all realized ones, all realized ones use the expressing of the Way. Just as the expressions of all realized ones are correctly transmitted, all realized ones correctly transmit the expressing of the Way. Accordingly, there is the insentient expressing of the Way, correctly transmitting from the ancient realized ones to the Past Seven Buddhas and from the Past Seven Buddhas to the present. All realized ones and all their ancestors exist within this insentient expressing of the Way. As for my present expressing of the Way, do not study it as if it were a new branch separate from the true transmission. As for the true transmission from the past, do not realize it as if it were an ancient nest or a demon's cave.

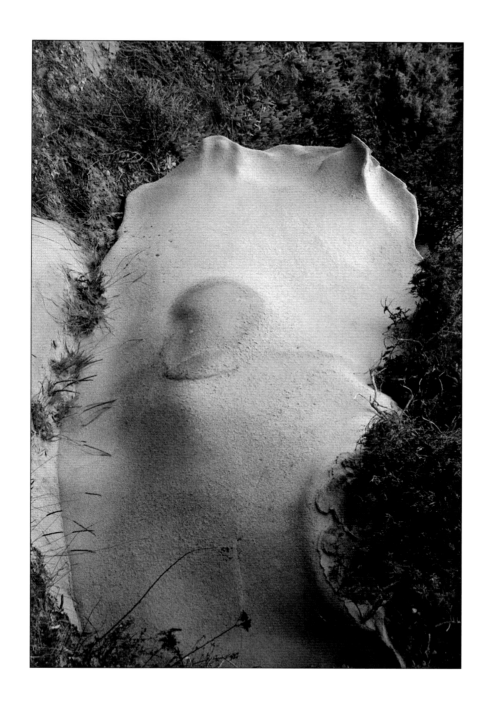

Commentary 2

Expressing the Way consists not only of 84,000 teachings; it has unlimited possibilities. It has infinite, limitless gates. There is a saying in Zen lore that says: "If all the waves of Caoxi were the same, people would drown on dry land." Caoxi was the home of the Sixth Ancestor of Zen, a great teacher who was the source of all currently existing Zen lineages. The waves that proceed from Caoxi are the successive generations of teachers that follow in these lineages. If their way of teaching was the same, "people would drown on dry land." Students would get stuck and become deluded, making a nest in the teachings. Teachers manifest the truth of reality in accord with their particular time, place, position, and degree. They must respond to the imperative they encounter.

Dogen says that an earlier expression of the teachings is not the same as a later expression. Yesterday's teachings are not expressed as today's teachings. That is why Shakyamuni Buddha said, "In the same way that the realized ones of the three existences expressed the Way, I, too, will now express a Way that is without distinctions." "Without distinctions" is intimacy. It's not yesterday, it's not tomorrow, it's not today— because in intimacy there is no yesterday, no tomorrow, no today.

The teachings of the insentient are also unique and appropriate to the circumstances. In effect, an important part of spiritual training is to be able to recognize the teachings whenever and however they may appear in this ever-changing flow and flux we call reality. Dew on the pine, the grasses and trees, the waves crashing on a rocky beach, a piece of kelp washed out at the tide line are all the real form of truth. They are the limitless life of the endless spring of enlightenment.

Most of us, however, miss this reality because of our habitual way of seeing and hearing, because of our preoccupation with what we know. We process only what fits within our reference system. Ultimately, this self-absorption results in a kind of blindness to anything new or unexpected.

We spend a lifetime honing and perfecting the aspect of our consciousness that is linear and sequential. Overpowered by words, ideas, positions, and understanding, the intuitive aspect of human consciousness is atrophied and all but forgotten. How do we go beyond that blindness, then? How do we go beyond the words and ideas that describe reality and directly experience and express the reality itself? When the mind settles down and we stop talking to ourselves, our intuition has the opportunity to open up and blossom.

Dogen is talking about making ourselves open and receptive to the teachings of the insentient. He is saying that the expression of the teachings by the insentient is no different than the teachings expressed from ancient times to the present by sages and realized ones. And that these teachings indeed exist within the inanimate's expression of the truth of the universe.

The way we normally respond to circumstances, the way we see ourselves, is based on our deep-seated patterns of conditioning. It is all learned behavior, a program we superimpose on what is actually happening. It took training to put it there. It takes time and patience to remove it. Layer by layer, we need to deal with that conditioning. Layer by layer, we peel it back, examining it, understanding it clearly, letting it go and going deeper. We do that until we reach the ground of being. That too, needs to be seen and then let go of. We simply keep going, just as reality keeps going. This practice is an endless process of seeing into wholeness. First, we see it within ourselves. Then, we see it in accord with the ten thousand things.

All realized ones and all their ancestors
  exist within this insentient expressing of the Way.

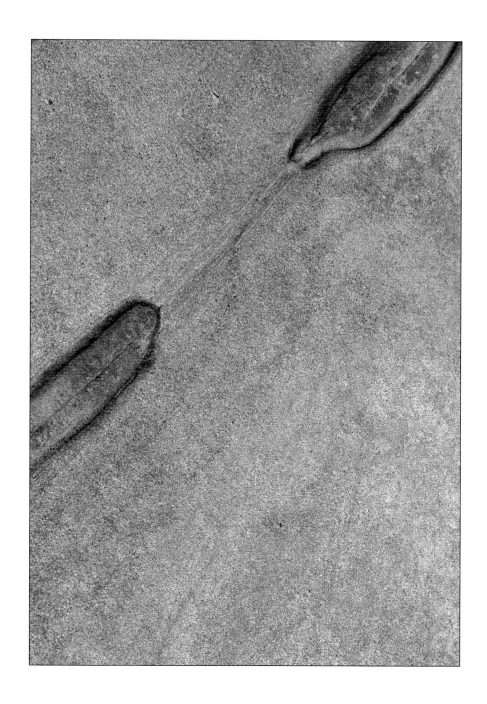

Once a monastic asked the Tang Dynasty Chinese National Teacher, Nanyang, "Do the insentient understand the expressing of the Way?" The National Teacher said, "They express the Way continually, energetically, ceaselessly." The monastic said, "Why can't I hear it?" The National Teacher replied, "The fact that you don't hear it has nothing to do with others hearing it." The monastic said, "I don't understand. What kind of person can hear it?" The National Teacher said, "All the holy ones can hear it." The monastic asked, "Do you hear it?" The National Teacher said, "I do not hear it." The monastic said, "If you do not hear it, how do you know that the insentient can express the Way?" The National Teacher said, "Fortunately I do not hear it. If I did, I would be one of the holy ones and you would not be able to hear me expressing the Way." The monastic said, "In that case, sentient beings can't hear it." The National Teacher said, "I express the Way for the sake of sentient beings, not for the sake of the holy ones." The monastic said, "Then what happens when sentient beings do hear you?" The National Teacher said, "At that moment they are not sentient beings."

Commentary 3

A single moment of yes and no
and heaven and earth are separated.
When all contriving is ended,
the whole is fully manifested.

Our usual way of understanding the insentient is as objects that make up the physical world, objects that are non-living, lacking consciousness or perception. They are stones, stars, atoms, mountains and rivers—the inanimate. On the other hand, we understand the sentient as the direct antithesis of the insentient; namely, as conscious, aware beings capable of responding to feeling and perception. Master Dogen's view is nondual. He sees the sentient and insentient as two parts of the same reality. He regards them as inseparable, as he does all dualities.

When we see reality in terms of separation, that process always begins with establishing the basic distinction between self and other. Then we extend that dualism to everything else that we see—good and bad, up and down, heaven and earth, black and white, sentient and insentient. Yet each and every duality is part of the same reality. Heads and tails are two sides of the same coin. One cannot exist without the other. How can you have the idea of "good" without the idea of "bad"? How can you talk of "up" unless there is a "down"? These pairs are mutually arising and interdependent.

This is a very different way of looking at the world, and of looking at the self and others. Appreciating the true nature of sentient and insentient beings from this all-encompassing perspective radically shifts our view. And it allows us to enter the realm where we may consider that the insentient—like the sentient—ceaselessly teach and express the truth of the universe.

In this section, Dogen is pointing to the boundless source of the teachings. Mountains and rivers are neither sentient nor insentient. The self is neither sentient nor insentient. When this is realized, the ten thousand things are the teacher, the teachings and the student. The ten thousand things are realized as the body of the universe—*your* body. Earth and living beings expound the truth. Water, birds and trees teach the truth. "These mountains and rivers of the present are a manifestation of the teachings of the ancient sages."

We should understand that this way of seeing is all-inclusive and we should not leave anything outside its scope. Cars, steel and cement sky-scrapers, the Brooklyn Bridge, are all proclaiming the truth as clearly and emphatically as a butterfly in its cocoon, a water-etched rock, and the robin's song. What then, we may ask, is the teaching of acid rain polluting our streams and lakes, of earthquakes, plague and pestilence? We should reflect on this matter, for there is something to be learned from each of these events.

Layman Dongpo was a renowned Chinese poet of antiquity. He once heard a sermon by a Zen teacher elaborating on the teachings of the insentient, but, despite his best efforts, he could never quite understand the full significance of it. Then, one night, he was suddenly awakened by the sound of the mountain stream flowing in the silence of the forest. At that moment, he attained enlightenment and composed the following poem:

Sounds of the streams are nothing but a
     great tongue;
The forms of mountains are none other
Than the Buddha's body of purity.
Eighty-four thousand verses since last night.
How shall I explain them tomorrow!

That night when Dongpo was enlightened by the sounds of the mountain stream, these sounds struck him as if raging torrents were soaring through the sky, obliterating everything. The sound of the stream became an all-encompassing discourse filling his whole body.

When there is no separation between subject and object, how can we speak from one point of view or another? The poet realized no separation. In truly hearing, he realized the teachings of the insentient that years of painstaking study did not reveal. But, in that moment of complete intimacy, who was enlightened—the poet, or the sound of the stream? Who is it that walks, you or the mountain?

The monastic questioning the National Teacher wanted to know why he could not hear the teaching of the insentient, and whether the National Teacher himself was able to hear it. When the National Teacher said he could not hear it, the monastic asked, "If you do not hear it, how do you know that the insentient can express the Way?" The National Teacher said, "Fortunately I do not hear it. If I did, you would not be able to hear me expressing the Way." The National Teacher was reaffirming that in order to hear the teachings of the insentient, there must be no gaps between sentient and insentient. He was saying that the insentient speak to and are heard by the insentient.

The monastic asked, "What happens when sentient beings do hear you?" The National Teacher said, "At that moment they are not sentient beings." Again, we can say that they are neither sentient nor insentient. This is the nondual realm of intimacy. It is here that this very body and mind, *your* very body and mind, is at once the body and mind of mountains and rivers and this great Earth itself.

A monastic asked,
   "What happens when sentient beings do hear you?"
The National Teacher said,
   "At that moment they are not sentient beings."

Whether they are beginners or advanced practitioners, those who wish to study the insentient expressing the Way should carefully study the teaching of this National Teacher. He said, "They express the Way continually, energetically, ceaselessly." "Continually" is the single moment within all time. Regarding the words "expressing ceaselessly," in the same way that "expressing" is already manifest, it necessarily is "ceaseless." Do not study this with the thought that the insentient expressing of the Way is just like the sentient. The realized Way does not fake the sounds of the insentient world by stealing the voices and sounds of the sentient world so that they resemble the sentient expressing the Way. The insentient expressing of the Way is not at all a physical sound heard with the ears, in the same way that the sentient expressing of the way is not a physical sound either.

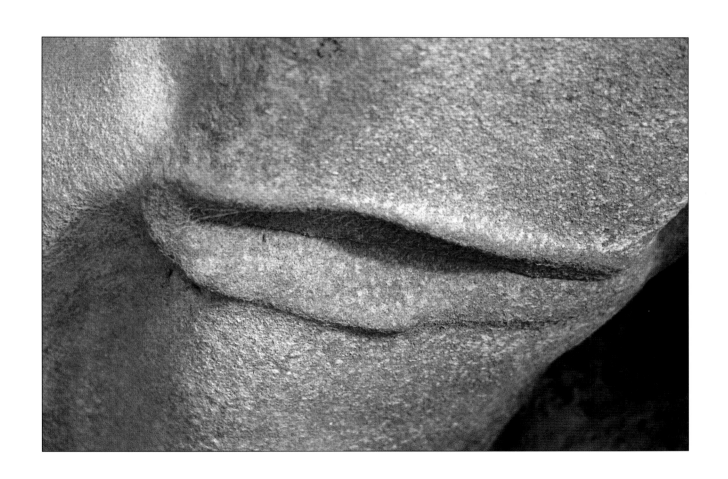

Commentary 4

Deaf, mute and blind—
already illuminating before it is said,
manifesting the body as preaching,
saving all sentient beings.

"They express the Way continually, energetically, ceaselessly." The expounding of the teachings does not stop for even an instant. How could it? How can the flow of existence—the sounds of the river valley, the forms of the boundless ocean—possibly come to a halt? Dogen says "continually" is the single moment within all time. This is the ceaseless practice of the existence of all things in this universe. It includes past, present and future. The reason this expression does not stop even for an instant, is that it's already present. It is beginningless and endless. This expression exists before there is a body and after the mind is forgotten. It exists in the time before our parents were born, and before the beginningless beginning of existence. It is not a matter for ordinary consciousness. How then, can it be heard?

When body and mind have fallen away, in the stillness that follows, the teachings are intimately manifested in great profusion. Whether we are aware of it or not, expression is always taking place.

The teaching of the insentient:
If you try to grasp it, you will miss it.
It has no form.
If you try to let go, you cannot separate from it.
It is not formless.

Subtle and wondrously inconceivable,
the muse constantly reveals the mysterious
teaching of the ten thousand things.

The teaching of the insentient: If you try to grasp it, you will miss it. It has no form. The insentient have form, but the teaching has no form. *If you try to let go, you cannot separate from it. It is not formless.* The teaching is not formless. If it has no form and it's not formless, what is it? If it's not sentient and it's not insentient, what is it? If it's not form and it's not emptiness, not existence or nonexistence, not being or non-being, then what is it? This is the essential matter for understanding the teachings.

Subtle and wondrously inconceivable, the muse constantly reveals the mysterious teaching of the ten thousand things. Unless you are ready to hear deeply, the insentient will not manifest anything but the superficial. But when you sit in meditation, quiet the mind, let go of all thoughts, and allow body and mind to fall away, the voice of the insentient will be heard.

One of the common pitfalls in attempting to understand the teachings of the insentient is our tendency to anthropomorphize nature.

Dogen says, "The realized Way does not fake the sounds of the insentient world by stealing the voices and sounds of the sentient world so that they resemble the sentient expressing the Way." As if the world was a Hollywood mega-production, we attribute our own human consciousness to the behavior and expressions of animals and wildlife. And by extension, we carry this interpretation into the world of the inanimate, applying human significance and judgment to a face in the clouds, the song of the cicada, or the "repulsive" smell of a skunk (which to a skunk is not repulsive at all).

Master Dogen says, "If you don't understand, it means to sanction a course of quietly learning in practice." If you don't understand it, just take the backward step. Just sit in the stillness of your own being. "If you do understand it, it means not to grasp it as intellectual understanding." That is our tendency. The minute we figure we have it, we name it. The minute we name it, it's no longer it. It's a name.

The teachings of the insentient cannot be perceived by the senses. When you are open and receptive, when you are alive and alert, everything is constantly teaching, constantly nourishing. These mountains and rivers, the great Earth and its boundless oceans are continually manifesting the words of the ancient teachers, continually expressing the truth of the universe. Indeed, if we examine this teaching carefully, we'll see that all phenomena—audible, inaudible, tangible and intangible, conscious and unconscious—are constantly expressing the truth. Sometimes you can't hear or see it, but they are expressing it. When you look for it, it can't be grasped, and yet it always comes home.

The insentient expressing of the Way
            is not at all a physical sound
heard with the ears.

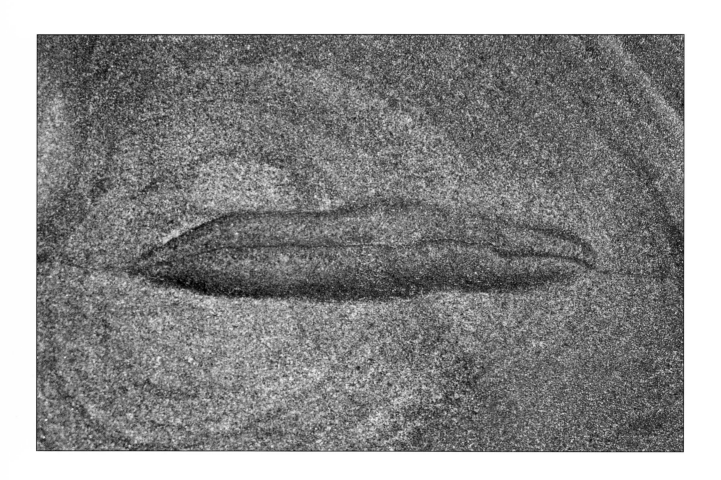

43

You should study diligently, asking yourself and asking others, "What is sentient? What is insentient?" You should study precisely and with all your heart the question of what is the meaning of the phrase "the insentient express the Way." The foolish conclude that the sound of branches in the forest or the opening of flowers and the falling of leaves are the insentient expressing the Way. They are not people who have studied the realized Way. If it were so, who would not know the insentient expressing the Way? Who would not hear the insentient expressing the Way? You should take time to turn a light on this. In the world of the insentient are there grasses, trees, and forests, or not? Is the world of the insentient blended in with the world of the sentient, or not? However, if you consider grasses, trees, tiles, and stones, and take them to be the insentient, this is limited knowledge. If you consider the concept "insentient," and take it to be grasses, trees, tiles, and stones, you have not arrived at fullness.

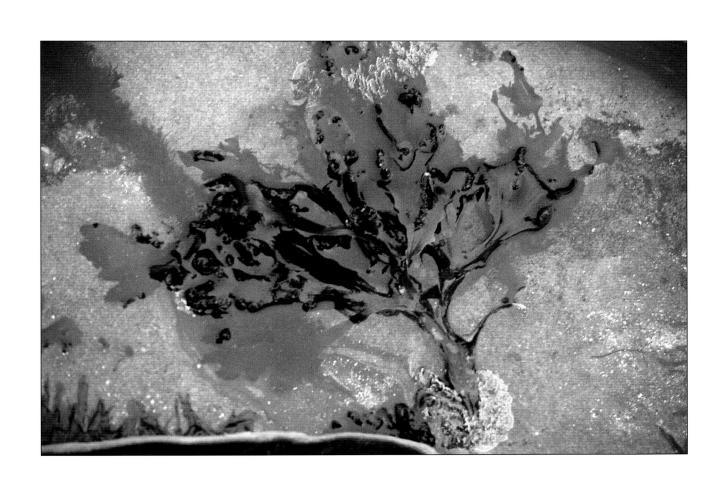

Commentary 5

It is at once you,
  yet you are not it.
It must be understood in this way,
  if you are to merge with thusness.

Although we have examined the ordinary meanings of sentient and insentient, here Dogen is asking us to study them in a much deeper way. He is essentially asking us *what is reality?* Is our reality the same as that of a rock, a bird or a caterpillar? If not, what makes it different?

In western psychology we speak of five senses—sight, hearing, taste, smell and touch. In Buddhist psychology there is an additional sensory dimension, which is thinking. Reality, as it's understood from a Buddhist perspective, is the coming together of the organ of perception, the object of perception, and consciousness. The reality of this book is dependent upon the visual perception of the organ: eye, the physical presence of the object: book, and consciousness. Because of the simultaneous presence of these three elements, we experience the reality: book. Close the eye, and the book is gone, even though consciousness and the physical book are still present. Remove the book, and it no longer exists, even though eye and consciousness exist. Remove consciousness (as in the experience of falling away of body and mind) and the reality of the book no longer exists.

Now, when we consider reality in which the organ of perception is mind and the object of perception is thought, we enter a different realm of understanding what we normally call "reality." For example, when we dream, we may experience in that dream state that we're being pursued by some unnamable creature. And as we run to escape it, our minds telegraph to our whole body the information we need in order to start running, despite the fact that our bodies are still reclined in sleep. Adrenaline begins to flow, our breathing becomes rapid, the general adaptation syndrome of fight or flight becomes activated, and we experience that dream state as if it were actually happening. If we suddenly awaken, we may find ourselves out of breath, dripping with sweat and trembling in fear until we realize with relief, "Oh! It was only a dream. It was just my mind that was creating this scenario." The fact is, it's just our mind that is creating the reality of our reading these words. It's just our mind that is doing everything we do.

The reality created by our minds has both subtle and profound effects on all aspects of our lives—our bodies, our perceptions, our actions. A good hypnotist can affect people's bodies simply by planting suggestions in their mind. For example, it is possible to put a subject under hypnosis and, while touching his forearm with a finger, suggest that he is being touched by a hot poker. Within seconds, a blister will appear. This is a involuntary reaction, an instinctive way in which the body protects itself against burns. Yet, the transformation is real, and it is brought about by the way the mind moves, by the reality it creates.

How we perceive ourselves and the universe directly affects the way we manifest in the world. With our mind, we can create clarity and confusion, we can create disease and health. Both possibilities exist, and many more. The human mind is incredibly powerful.

In view of this way of understanding, we can set aside our dictionary definitions of "sentient" and "insentient." Then, when we see a rock in its thusness—that is, not from our self-centered point of view, but rather from the perspective of the rock—there can be little doubt that the resulting reality will be very different from what we habitually experience. The same is true when we examine the phrase "the insentient express the Way." It should be clear that this kind of expression goes far beyond the sound of the wind in the pines, or the opening of flowers and the falling of leaves. Indeed, as Dogen says, if we regard the world of the insentient as being grasses, trees, and forest, we limit our understanding. And if we regard their world as being some sort of blending of sentient and insentient, we miss the reality of both. The reality of this expression of the teachings

is not sentient, nor is it insentient. Nor is it neither, or both. It simply exists *thus!* Dogen says in the "Mountains and Rivers Sutra:"

What different types of beings see is different, and we should reflect on this fact. Is it that there are various ways of seeing one object? Or is it that we have mistaken various images for one object? We should concentrate every effort on understanding this question, and then concentrate still more.

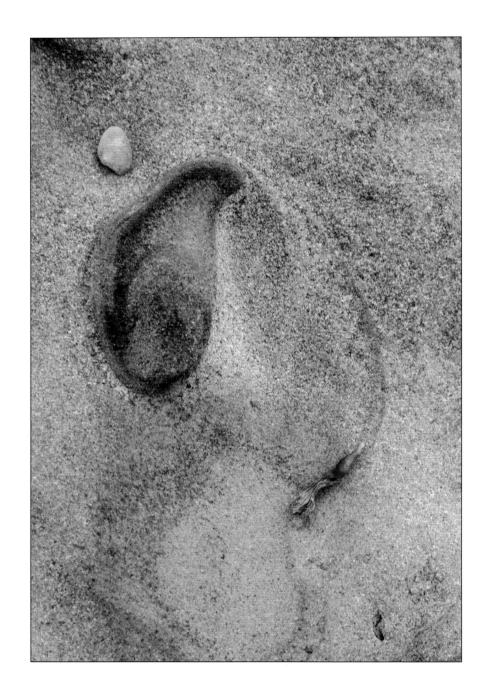

Is the world of the insentient
     the grasses, trees, and forests, or not?
Is the world of the insentient blended in
     with the world of the sentient, or not?

Even if we were to take the grasses, trees, and so forth that people see and regard them as insentient, grasses and trees are not matters for ordinary thinking to determine. Consider some of the reasons. Forests in the world of heavenly beings are clearly special, and not at all the same as the forests of China and its environs. Grasses and trees of the sea are different from the grasses and trees of the mountains. Moreover, the sky has forests, clouds have forests, and hundreds of grasses and thousands of trees are born and mature amid fire and wind. In general there are those that have been studied as sentient; there are those that have not been taken as insentient. Some grasses and trees are human-like or animal-like. The sentient and insentient are not yet clarified. When it comes to the trees, rocks, flowers, fruits and water of the hermits, for example, even when they do not doubt what they see, it is hard for them to explain it in words. Don't conclude with a categorization that says that because you saw some of the grasses and trees of China, and because you are familiar with the grasses and trees of Japan, the inexhaustible worlds in all directions must be like this too.

Commentary 6

It's not like reflections in a mirror or echoes in the valley—
when you really see, you go blind,
when you really hear, you go deaf.

Our way of perceiving and understanding the universe is of necessity determined by our human characteristics. Compared to other species, we have some advantages just by virtue of being human, but we also have some physical limitations. Unlike the owl, we can only see a narrow band of the electromagnetic spectrum. We can only hear a particular range of sound frequencies, and are deaf to those that are audible to the bat or the wolf. What we see, hear, feel, taste, and touch defines our experience of the universe. When we couple this with our intelligence and reasoning ability, our worldview becomes particularly defined.

With human communication being what it is, most humans subscribe to essentially the same worldview—what Dogen calls "ordinary thinking." But when we can step out of that conditioned way of seeing and experiencing the universe, we find that, as Dogen says in the "Mountains and Rivers Sutra:"

In general… the way of seeing mountains and rivers differs according to the type of being that sees them. There are beings who see what we call water as a jeweled necklace… or, again they see water as miraculous flowers… hungry ghosts see water as raging flames or as pus and blood. Dragons and fish see it as a palace or a tower.

Clearly, how different types of beings see is different.

A spider web is a spider's whole universe. A spider can "see" and experience the world as far as her web reaches. She is aware of anything that comes into contact with that web, and instantly knows where and what it is. She recognizes the difference between a drop of rain and a fly that has landed on the web, and she knows their precise location, which allows her to respond accordingly. A caterpillar differentiates between trees, distinguishing a pine tree, a maple tree, an oak. It doesn't eat pine trees; it eats maple trees. On the other hand, the robin that sits in the tree doesn't care about what kind of tree it's sitting on. To make that distinction does not impart anything to its wellbeing and survival. But it clearly notices what kind of caterpillar is crawling on the bark of the tree.

Then there are the infinite versions of the way humans see an object—a tree, for instance. What, indeed, is a tree? The reason you call it a "tree" may be that when you were young, your mother pointed to one and said, "Tree." And you said, "Kree?" And she said, "No, no, dear, *tree*." And you got it. When physical chemists look at a tree, they might see a conglomerate of cellulose molecules, hydrogen and carbon linking together. Biologists might see a specific species of tree. Ecologists might see it in terms of its relationship to the environment, the water it is processing, the oxygen it's releasing and the CO_2 it's absorbing. There's the artistic reality of that tree, where conventions of language, classifications and culture are thrown away. In Joyce Kilmer's celebrated poem, his tree "looks at God all day and lifts her leafy arms to pray." Then there is Van Gogh's way of seeing a tree. Dogen says, "Moreover, the sky has forests, clouds have forests."

Given this multitude of perspectives, it follows that the training on the way of practice and verification must also not be merely of one or two kinds, and the ultimate realm must also have a thousand types and ten thousand kinds.

Inherent in each one of us is the potential of perceiving the universe in limitless ways. We should learn to give rein to our perception and allow the ceaseless teachings of the ten thousand things to be perceived clearly and intimately.

The sky has forests,
      clouds have forests,
and hundreds of grasses and thousands of trees
      are born and mature amid fire and wind.

The National Teacher said, "All the holy ones can hear it." He said that among the disciples of the insentient expressing the Way, all the holy ones stand on the ground and listen. The holy ones and the insentient together actualize hearing, and bring about the actualization of expressing. The insentient express the Way for the sake of all holy ones. Are the insentient holy? Are they ordinary? Those who have finally clarified the meaning of the insentient expressing the Way fully embody that which is heard by all the holy ones. Once you attain this embodiment, you will know how to identify the realm of the holy ones. Moreover, you should study thoroughly the walk along the night path that transcends both the holy and the ordinary.

The National Teacher, Nanyang, said, "I do not hear it." Do not take this as something that is easy to understand. Does he not hear because he has surpassed the ordinary and gone beyond the holy? Does he not hear because he has broken open the ordinary and the holy, the nest and the cave? Make an effort in this way and you will actualize his teaching.

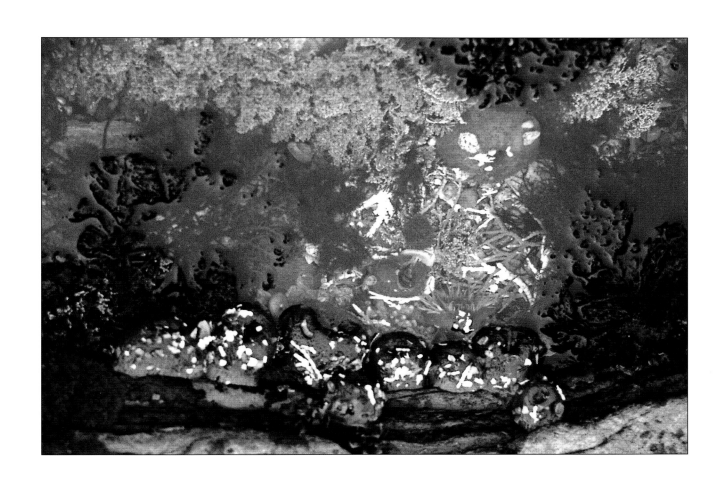

Commentary 7

Riding the winding river deep into the night,
both banks dissolve in darkness.
Being found by the wonder of the flow,
my way opens of its own.

All the sages standing on the ground hear the insentient expounding the teachings. "Standing on the ground" was the traditional way of hearing a formal discourse in the monasteries of China and Japan. It implies total presence, openness and receptivity. It's not casual listening. But Dogen says both the sages *and* the insentient actualize hearing, and bring about the actualization of expressing. That is, both the hearing and expressing are the cause *and* the effect. From the perspective of nonduality, cause does not precede effect, nor does effect follow cause. Cause and effect are a single entity. The holy ones and the insentient are a single reality, totally interdependent, mutually arising and with a mutual causation. Yet one does not hinder the other.

When a photographer is in complete communion with his or her subject, to a point where both subject and photographer have merged in a single thusness, the camera photographs by itself. What is the cause of the photograph? Is it the photographer, the subject, the camera? Is it all three? Or is it none of them?

Who are the holy ones that Dogen speaks of? And why are they the only ones who can hear the teachings of the insentient? Are they different from ordinary beings? Do they possess some special kind of hearing and seeing that makes them sages? The state of consciousness that a sage possesses is no different from that which each one of us already embodies. We are born with the potential to see this truth, and we will die with it. When that fact is realized, we enter the realm of the sage. Dogen then takes this exploration a step further and asks that we "study thoroughly the walk along the night path that transcends both the holy and the ordinary."

"Night" is a metaphor for the absolute basis of reality, and to walk along the "night path" is to function in that realm in which all dualistic distinctions dissolve, in which the difference between sacred and profane is transcended. Taking the backward step of meditation is the gateway to the night path. In the stillness of meditation, we watch the flow of thoughts coming and going. Little by little, through constant awareness of that flow, the internal dialogue that constantly reaffirms our sense of "self" gradually diminishes, until we reach a point where the thoughts disappear. When the thoughts disappear, the thinker disappears. Thought and thinker are interdependent entities, two parts of the same reality. One cannot exist without the other. When the thinker disappears, the night path becomes evident. The self-centeredness that normally dominates our way of seeing and hearing shifts. However, reaching this place can be a dead end, unless that which is realized along the night path is actualized in the light of day.

Zhaozhou asked Master Touzi, "How is it when a person who has died the great death comes to life?" Touzi said, "They should not go by night. They must arrive in daylight."

Realization of the unity of all things must ultimately be manifested in the world of differences. The absolute emptiness of all things is exactly the form of all phenomena. Therefore, "surpassing the ordinary and going beyond the holy" is that which exists *thus*.

The National Teacher said, "All the holy ones can hear." Since both the holy ones and the insentient can hear the teachings of the insentient, why does the National Teacher say, "I don't hear it"? Is it because he is not a sage? Is it because he is not insentient? Or is it because, as Dogen suggests, "He has surpassed the ordinary and gone beyond the holy"? Or is it because "He has broken open the ordinary and the holy, the nest and the cave"?

We must remember that hearing the teachings of the insentient is a matter of intimacy, of nonduality. Only the insentient can hear the teachings of the insentient. Only sages are intimate with the insentient. In ordinary relationships, there is a clear distinction between the sentient and the insentient. In intimacy, there is none. Therefore, if the National Teacher heard the insentient, then the questioning monastic would be incapable of hearing him, since the monastic is still functioning in the realm of this and that.

In "Genjokoan," Master Dogen says, "Seeing forms with the whole body and mind, hearing sounds with the whole body and mind, one understands them intimately." It is this whole body and mind intimacy that is at work in hearing the insentient.

You should study thoroughly
        the walk along the night path
that transcends both the holy and the ordinary.

The National Teacher said, "Fortunately I do not hear it. If I did, I would be a holy one." What he is pointing to here is not just some words. "Fortunately I" is not ordinary or holy. Is "fortunately I" a realized one? Because the realized ones have surpassed the ordinary and gone beyond the holy, that which they hear is certainly not the same as what all holy ones hear.

By cultivating the logic of the National Teacher's words, "Then you would not hear me expressing the Way," you can practice the enlightened wisdom of all realized ones and all holy ones. The key point is that all holy ones can hear the insentient expressing the Way. We practitioners can hear the National Teacher expressing the Way. Make an effort to study this teaching throughout the days, throughout the months. You should take the time to ask the National Teacher, "I don't ask about the time after all beings hear, but what about the exact moment when all beings hear the expressing of the Way?"

Master Dongshan, when he was studying under Master Yunyan, asked him, "The insentient express the Way. What kind of person can hear it?" Yunyan replied, "The insentient express the Way, and the insentient can hear it." Dongshan asked, "Do you hear it, or not?" Yunyan replied, "If I heard it, you would not be able to hear me expressing the Way." Dongshan said, "If that's the case, then I do not hear you expressing the Way." Yunyan said, "I am expressing it and still you do not hear. How much less likely that you will hear the insentient expressing the Way." Dongshan composed this verse and offered it to Yunyan, saying:

> *How extraordinary! How extraordinary!*
> *The insentient express the Way! How mysterious!*
> *If you listen with the ears, it is incomprehensible.*
> *If you hear sounds with the eyes, it is truly knowable.*

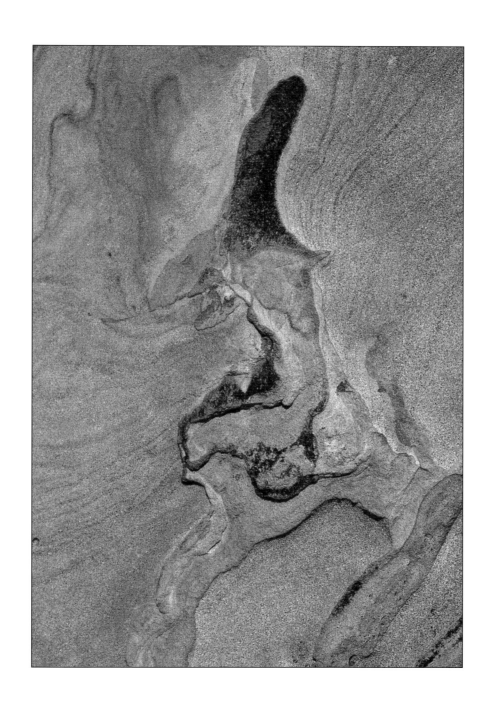

Commentary 8

*Vertically extending through
past, present, and future.
Horizontally spreading,
covering the ten directions.*

The National Teacher said, "Fortunately I do not hear it. If I did, I would be a holy one." Whose good fortune is this—the monastic's or the insentient's? Let's say we appreciate the intimacy that exists between the sages and the insentient—the intimacy that is required for the teachings of the insentient to be heard. Doesn't it naturally follow that there should be some degree of intimacy between the National Teacher and the monastic, if the monastic is to hear the teachings of the National Teacher? This is what Dogen means when he says that this teaching is "not just some words." He is saying that the National Teacher's expression of the Way is a total expression of the Way adapted to the imperative of time, place, position and degree. In this case, the expression is adjusted for the monastic to understand it.

In questioning, each one of us comes from a particular viewpoint. This, in turn, affects our ability to hear the answer. The National Teacher adjusted his answer to meet the monastic's question, at the same time avoiding intellectual explanations that could have easily turned into a nest of words. Therefore, the National Teacher's problem is how to awaken this questioning monastic who, by virtue of the sincerity of his question, is "standing on the ground," prepared to receive the teachings. The National Teacher must awaken within the monastic the realization that he already embodies the ability to hear the expression of the Way by the insentient, just as the sages do. As practitioners we can hear the National Teacher expounding the teachings. As sages, we can hear the insentient expounding the teachings. Are these two the same, or are they different?

In transmitting the teachings, there is neither explanation nor is there teaching. There is neither hearing nor attainment. Since explanation never really explains anything, nor is it able to teach, why talk about it? Since listening isn't really hearing or attaining anything, then why listen? Since it can neither be explained nor heard, how is it possible to help someone enter the Way?

*When reasoning is exhausted,
body and mind fall away.
When the defilement of things is eliminated,
the light first appears.*

The great matter, which is the experience of surpassing the ordinary and going beyond the holy, is not contained in practice nor attained after enlightenment. It is simply that when you speak about it, you cannot hear it. Dogen says, "You should take the time to ask the National Teacher, 'I don't ask about the time after all beings hear, but what about the exact moment when all beings hear the expressing of the Way?'" I say, you should ask yourself about the exact moment when all beings hear the expressing of the Way. The exact moment has no before, and it has no after. The moment arrives as it departs, simultaneously. The moment is where our life takes place. If we miss the moment, we have missed our lives. Unfortunately, because of our preoccupation with the past—which doesn't exist; it's already happened—or the future—which doesn't exist; it hasn't happened yet—we miss the moment, and therefore, we miss our lives. Life slips by and we barely notice it in passing.

The process of meditation trains the mind to be present in the moment-to-moment reality of existence. We challenge ourselves to be present to our own breathing, and when our mind drifts away, we acknowledge the thought that has carried it astray, and bring our attention back to where we want it, to the breath. As this skill develops and deepens our attentiveness, we find that our awareness of the things we encounter each day becomes heightened. We prepare ourselves to "stand on the ground" and receive the teachings.

Dogen then introduces the dialogue between Yunyan and his student Dongshan, which takes place about a hundred and fifty years later, and which enters the same ground as the dialogue between the National teacher and the questioning monastic. In this case, there is, however, a subtle shift. When Dongshan asked Yunyan, "Do you hear the insentient expressing the Way?" Yunyan replied, "If I heard it, you would not be able to hear me expressing the Way." This answer follows the response of the National Teacher to the monastic. However, Dongshan, unlike the monastic said, "In that case, I do not hear you expressing the Way." This statement was Dongshan's expression of his realization of the insentient expressing the Way. Yunyan's saying, "I am expressing it, and still you do not hear me," is his way of verifying Dongshan's hearing of the teachings of the insentient. Dongshan is essentially saying, "The insentient express the Way, and it can be heard only by the insentient" and, "I do not hear you expressing the Way."

We should study this dialogue carefully, for it contains the heart of the correct transmission of the Way from generation to generation.

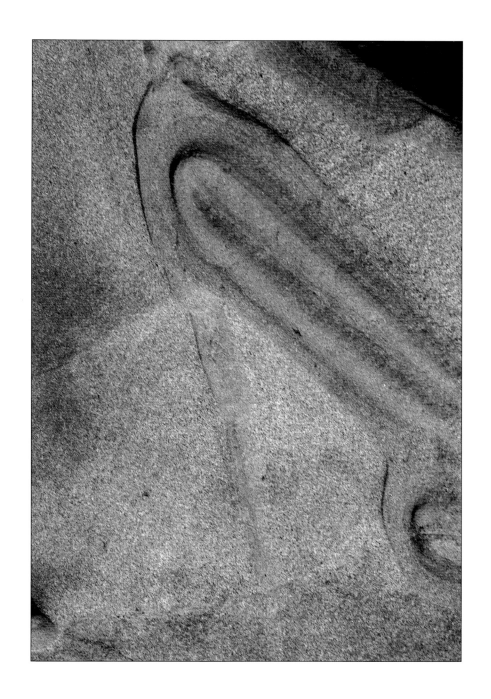

Now, with regard to this teaching of Master Dongshan, "What kind of person can hear the insentient expressing the Way," you should make a good and careful investigation through this life and many lives.
This question also provides the virtue and benefit of a teaching. This teaching has skin, flesh, bones and marrow. It is not only the mind being transmitted by the mind. Mind being transmitted by mind is the practice and affirmation of both beginners and advanced practitioners. There is a barrier key that is correctly transmitted by the offering of the robe, and that is correctly transmitted by the raising of the teaching. Present day people—how can they reach the ultimate in only three or four years of effort?

Though it is said that Dongshan had heard and seen the main point of Nanyang's earlier statement that "all holy ones can hear the insentient expressing the Way," there is now, additionally, his question—"What kind of person can hear the insentient expressing the Way?" Do you take this as affirming Nanyang's statement? Do you take it as denying Nanyang's statement? Do you take it as a question? Do you take it as a statement? If it completely denies Nanyang, how do you take Dongshan's words? If it completely affirms Nanyang, then how do you understand Dongshan's words?

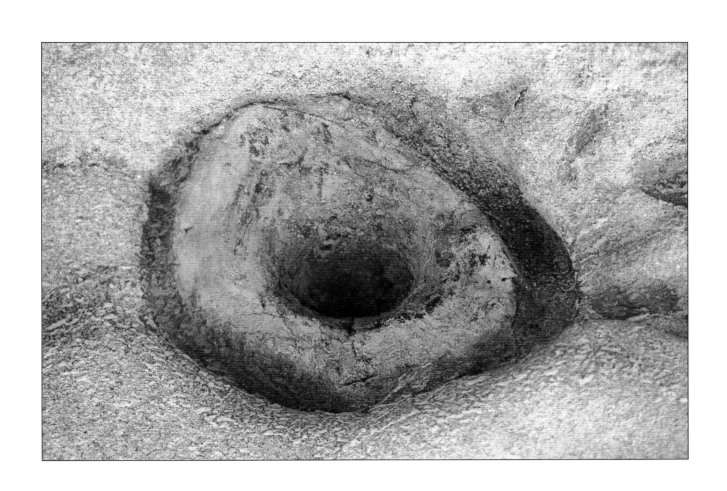

Commentary 9

Parent and child become each other,
they become each other.
Before spring has arrived,
the fragrance of blossoms fills the valley.

Master Dogen begins this section with the statement that Dongshan's question "What kind of person can hear the insentient expressing the Way?" is, in actual fact, a teaching. How is it a teaching? And what kind of teaching is it? Dogen exhorts us to "make a good and careful investigation through this life and many lives." What is he asking? It has already been stated that when the monastic was questioning the National Teacher, saying, "What kind of person can hear it?" the National Teacher said, "All the holy ones can hear it." Who are the holy ones? What is the virtue and benefit of this question—indeed, of any question?

The path of authentic spiritual practice can be rigorous and far-reaching. The long training needed to clarify one's life and the nature of the universe requires a continuous effort of studying and refining one's insights and realizations as to the true nature of what we habitually call the self. In the Zen tradition, this kind of study includes deep meditation, the practice of liturgy, the taking up of moral and ethical teachings, and exploring and digesting hundreds of koans. And throughout this process, there are repeated encounters with a teacher who is constantly testing, probing, pointing, and demanding nothing short of an authentic expression of the truth of this life. This is a process that can be very powerful and transforming. But it's not yet the mind being transmitted by mind.

My own teacher had students who trained with him for many years. They completed all of the rigors of formal training and finished koan study, yet in several cases, he did not authenticate the transmission of the teachings. Why? Something else needs to happen. It's not enough to just receive information—not even to train rigorously. It is not a matter of understanding or believing the teachings. Most importantly, transmission is not dependent on anything passing from one person to another. Rather, there must be an acknowledgment of a teacher-student identification, in which the teacher's and the student's experiences are in complete accord, fundamentally originating in one and the same truth. When this truth is realized, it transforms the way we perceive ourselves and the universe. It arises from within us. It is not something that is given or received.

Mind-to-mind transmission and the teachings of the insentient occur because, from the very beginning, we are intrinsically clear. Because, from the beginning, we are already endowed with the capacity to hear with the eye and see with the ear. Each and every one of us has this ability, this nature. Every single one of us is perfect, complete, and lacking nothing. Yet, for each of us, our particular conditioning is different, as is our personal causality. Therefore, the things we need to work through are different. There is no way to realize our inherent freedom and perfection if we hold on to our conditioning. Any attachment, no matter how small, separates heaven from earth, teacher from student, the self from the universe. As long as there is holding on, there will always be the self that is holding on, and body and mind cannot possibly fall away.

In examining a question deeply, with the whole body and mind, it becomes a teaching that has skin, flesh, bones and marrow. It is not only mind being transmitted by mind, but the body itself becoming a vehicle of the truth and expressing it in every single activity.

We must now ask, what is the "barrier key that is correctly transmitted by the offering of the robe, and that is correctly transmitted by the raising of the teaching?" Dongshan, although he had seen and heard the main point of Nanyang's, "All the holy ones can hear the insentient expressing the Way," nevertheless took the statement much deeper by inquiring, "What kind of person can hear the insentient expressing the Way?"

We should understand that a genuine practitioner exhaustively investigating the teachings, will find—quite unexpectedly—by neither the efforts of the mind nor the strengths of the body, that the teachings come home to her consciousness, as if of their own accord. The question, the great doubt, provides the cutting edge.

It cannot be described,
it cannot be pictured.
The beauty of this garden is invisible
even to the great sages.

Mind being transmitted by mind
        is the practice and affirmation
of both beginners and advanced practitioners.

Dongshan's teacher, Yunyan, said, "The insentient express the Way, and the insentient can hear it." Correctly transmitting this lineage, there is study by means of the dropping away of body and mind. This statement, "the insentient express the Way, and the insentient can hear it" is identical to "all realized ones express the Way and all realized ones are able to hear it." An assembly that would listen to the insentient expressing the Way, whether it is composed of sentient beings or insentient beings, whether it is made up of ordinary people or wise and holy ones, would be an assembly of the insentient. By means of this complete reality, one can distinguish truth from falsehood both in the past and in the present. Even if a teacher arrives from India, if he is not an authentic teacher of the true transmission, you should not follow him. Even if something was practiced continuously for one thousand or ten thousand years, if it was not mutually passed from heir to heir, it will be hard to carry on. Today the true transmission is well known in China and it should be easy to distinguish what is true and what is false. If you listen to the teaching, "All beings express the Way, and all beings can hear it," you will receive the bones and marrow of all the realized ones and all their ancestors.

Commentary 10

If you still don't understand,
look at September, look at October—
leaves of red and gold
cover the mountain and fill the valley.

"The insentient express the Way, and the insentient can hear it" is identical to "All realized ones express the Way, and all realized ones are able to hear it."

The ability to hear the expression of the insentient is implicit in the insentient. Therefore, only the insentient can hear the expression of the insentient. It has been shown, that in the transmission of the teachings, nothing goes from teacher to student. Instead, there is the student's realization of the truth, which is none other than the truth realized by the teacher. In Zen, this is traditionally expressed as "buddhas transmit to buddhas." The insentient communicate with the insentient. Therefore, it follows that "an assembly that would listen to the insentient expressing the Way… would be an assembly of the insentient." We should ask the question, what is the nature of the communication when we can really hear the teachings of the insentient? Or when a teacher and student make a genuine mind-to-mind connection? One way to get some insight into this process is to consider the nature of resonance.

In physics, resonance is the coupling of two vibrational frequencies. The classic example is the resonance between a pair of tuning forks. One fork is struck and begins to vibrate, emitting a sound. When the second fork is brought into the vicinity of the first one, the energy of the already vibrating fork is transmitted to the second fork through open space, and it starts vibrating at the same frequency. This coupling is only possible if the natural frequency of the second fork corresponds to that of the first one. In other words, from the beginning, both forks contain the capacity to make the same sound. The phenomenon of resonance is present, not only in the coupling of sound frequencies, but also in light and water waves, molecules, and atoms.

This principle—the manifestation of an intrinsic connection or identity between two apparently separate entities—is an essential aspect of the mind-to-mind transmission in spiritual practice, and of the appreciation of some of the mystic dimensions of reality. It is also of fundamental importance in the creative process. When it is functioning at its best, it opens a gateway that provides an intimate connection between art, artist and subject, allowing that experience of intimacy to manifest as artistic expression. By extension, when we consider this resonance in relationship to the insentient expressing the Way, it becomes clear that the possibility exists for direct, immediate communication to take place, provided the natural frequencies are in accord.

I find that in my photography work, I rely on resonance with a subject—whether sentient or insentient—to guide me to levels of interaction that are simply not present on the surface. The images in this book are the result of a single, intensive day of photographing at Point Lobos, California, a mecca for many artists who consider photography a sacred art.

When I arrived at Point Lobos, I headed for a bowl-shaped cove peppered with small islands. Sitting there, in the midst of the sounds of the sea and the wind whistling through the rocks' crevasses, layers of mental noise began to fall away. My impressions of my plane ride to the West Coast, the airport, the city, its highways, their sounds and smells slowly dissolved until there was only the immediacy of that beach and its insentient inhabitants.

Then the resonance began and the dance unfolded. As my senses cleared, images began to reveal themselves—gradually at first, then more and more intensely, until they seemed to be rushing at me. They could not be ignored. Golden kelp floating in a purple tidal pool, wet rocks splashed with lichen graffiti, bone bleached shells lying on a bed on multi-colored pebbles. The images kept appearing and disappearing, accompanied by the symphony of the surf, sea lions and wind.

As I photographed, I did not try to recognize or name what the camera was seeing. It was as if subject, camera and I were connected by a thread that made my sense of sight and communication instant and intimate. What is this thread? Can it be named? Is it resonance? Inspiration? The Muse? Does it even matter what it's called? I ask you, can there be any doubt that all beings express the Way, and all beings can hear it? Furthermore, is this expression one, or is it two?

All beings express the Way,
      and all beings can hear it.

If you hear the words of Yunyan and listen to the words of Nanyang, and truly take them in, you will know that "all the holy ones" in the statement "All the holy ones can hear," are insentient, and you will know that "the insentient" in the statement "the insentient can hear" are all holy ones. This is because that which the insentient express is insentient, and the insentient expressing the Way is itself insentient. In other words, the insentient express the Way, and the expressing of the Way is insentient.

Dongshan said, "If that's the case, then I do not hear you expressing the Way." This phrase, "If that's the case," highlights the main point of Yunyan's statement "The insentient express the Way, and the insentient can hear it." In accordance with the teaching that "The insentient express the Way, and the insentient can hear it," comes "I do not hear you expressing the Way." With these words Dongshan did not just touch the edge of the seat of the insentient expressing the Way, he struck the sky by making apparent his intentions towards the insentient expressing the Way. This is not just fully accomplishing the insentient expressing the Way, it is fully investigating both hearing and not hearing the insentient expressing the Way. Going further, he brought about the full accomplishment of expressing, not expressing, past expressing, present expressing, and future expressing of the sentient expressing the Way. Moreover, in the end he also clarified the teaching that hearing and not hearing the expressing of the Way are both sentient and insentient.

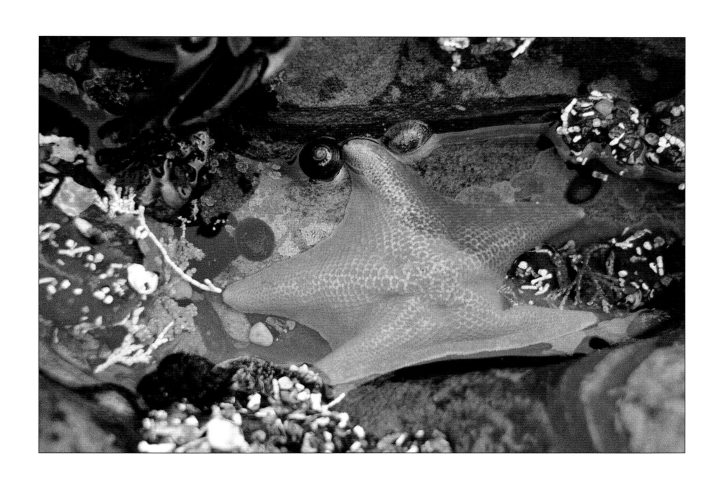

Commentary *11*

Vast and boundless,
        open and free—there are no gaps.
Who are the sentient beings,
        who are the buddhas?

"That which the insentient express is insentient." To understand the teachings of the rock, we have to *be* the rock. To understand the teachings of the universe, we have to recognize the identity of the universe and this self. To hear the instructions of ancient masters we have to identify with their mind. To benefit from the teachings of our life, we have to be intimate with our life. This means that we have to get out of the way of our life, we have to let go of the ideas about what that life is and what the self is. We have to trust life and give it permission to live itself.

Life is a creative process that is happening in this present moment. The only reality we have is the present moment. The objective of spiritual practice is to close the gap between reality and what we think is real. When we succeed in letting go of our notions of the self, we become one with our lives, one with this moment. There is no self, no other, no this or that. The universe exists in its entirety within each moment. This is what it means to forget the self—to see that there is, in fact, no self. To live knowing that there is no self is what in Zen is called the action of non-action. Our activity, regardless of its nature, is allowed to flow by itself. It develops spontaneously, without forcing or straining—like the way we grow our hair. There is no deliberate intent whatsoever. Reality advances and realizes

the self. This is: "That which the insentient express is insentient."

In art, when the artist has stepped out of the way, the brush paints by itself, the camera photographs by itself, the dance dances by itself. There is no reflection, hesitation, or self-consciousness. There is just the complete expression of that event, of that meeting. The creative process, like the workings of a spiritual journey, points us towards our essential nature, which is a reflection of the boundless creativity of the universe.

When we step out of the way, our life pours through us; the universe pours through us. We might have had chance experiences that confirm that for us, moments of insight and grace—epiphanies—and we may conclude that we were somehow fortunate or spiritually talented. The fact is that these occurrences do not happen to us. We create them in the same way that we create the universe—through intimacy.

Seeing form with the whole body and mind, hearing sound with the whole body and mind, liberates us. It helps us realize the freedom that has always been there. Having realized that intimacy, we are unhindered in our relationship with this Earth and all of its beings. That is the intimacy that Dogen challenges us with when he says, "This is not just fully accomplishing the insentient expressing the Way, it is fully investigating both hearing and not hearing the insentient expressing the Way." To see and to hear—indeed, to live—with the whole body and mind is the ability to "ride the clouds and to follow the wind."

Yet, this is nothing special. This is the potential of every human being. We are born with it, just as we are born with the ability to walk, laugh and cry. It is called our true nature. This true nature is the nature of all sentient and insentient beings. But it is buried, concealed beneath the layers of conditioning that we have accumulated from time immemorial. In each one of us lives an enlightened being, and the most important thing each one of us can ever do with our lives is to realize that, to make that enlightened being real as a free expression of our lives. When we do that, we make ourselves free, and that freedom is then actualized in everything we do: in the way we drive a car, grow a garden, prepare a meal, program a computer, raise a child, live a life, and die.

The insentient express the Way,
        and the expressing of the Way
is insentient.

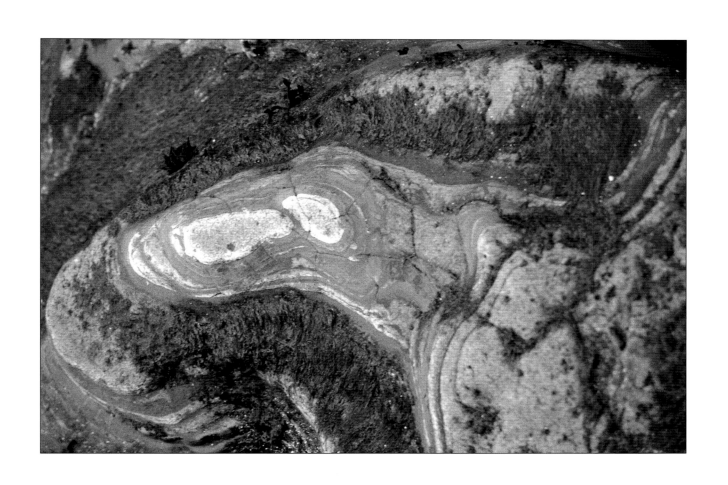

In general, hearing the teachings of the Way is not just a matter of physical hearing or conscious hearing. It is hearing the teachings with all force, all mind, all body, all speech, from as far in the past as before your father and mother were born, before the first sound in the universe, up to the limit of the future and the unlimited future beyond that. It is hearing the teachings before the body and after the mind. These ways of hearing the teachings always have benefits. Do not say that there is no benefit in hearing the teachings unless the hearing is conditioned by consciousness. Even those whose minds are not operating and whose bodies have collapsed can obtain benefit from hearing the teachings. Those without minds and without bodies can obtain benefit from hearing the teachings. All realized ones and all ancestors without fail spent time like this, and in so doing they created realized ones and became ancestors. How can ordinary thinking completely comprehend that the power of the teachings touches the body and the mind? Ordinary thinking is unable by itself to completely clarify the limits of body and mind.

Commentary 12

To look for a form or search for a sound
is to stumble down the wrong path.
The wisdom that cannot be taught,
alone reveals that which is enduring and real.

Ordinary thinking cannot fathom the teachings of the insentient, the teachings of the enlightened ones, these teachings of Dogen. Ordinary thinking cannot comprehend our own enlightened nature. A thought is an abstraction of reality. It is a word-image, not the direct experience of the object it captures in its description. For example, take the word "hit." When you look at it on the written page, what you see is a collection of letters. If you close your eyes and say "hit," you hear the word. But if I hit you—that is a direct experience, a complete body and mind event that includes the totality of this moment.

In Zen lore there are innumerable examples of exchanges between students and masters where a query about the fundamental aspect of reality is responded to with a shout or a blow with a staff. The words and concepts through which we filter reality are like a box we have locked ourselves in. Our whole vision of reality comes out of those words and concepts. And we are not even aware that this is what is going on.

When a child asks a question, we answer it with a word, and so the child begins to confuse that word with reality. "What is rain?" "It is water falling from the sky." But that does not convey what rain really is. We make assumptions and conclude that we understand something

because we can name it. As a result, most of us go through life confusing the true appreciation of what things are with mere names and descriptions. In order to appreciate the reality, we need to go beyond words, or to the place and time "before words." We need to access the direct experience of reality itself. That is the realm of the wisdom that has no teacher, the wisdom from "before your father and mother were born," the teachings from "before the body and after the mind."

Words have meaning. Life does not have meaning. Rain does not have meaning. Mountains and rivers do not have meaning. The self has no meaning. Take away the words and there is no meaning, just the experience—the experience of the rain, of the tree, of the self, of reality. Dogen is trying to tell us that there are teachings which are not necessarily conditioned by consciousness. Even in the darkness of not knowing, illumination is active and functioning. Indeed, in the words of an ancient scripture:

Within light there is darkness,
but do not try to understand that darkness.
Within darkness there is light,
but do not look for that light.

Light and darkness are a pair,
like the foot before and the foot behind in walking.

It is clear that we cannot really explain this life, but we can experience its boundless perfection. It is in this immediate experience that we see, hear, taste, touch, and feel the boundless perfection of both the sentient and insentient. It is here that we can abide in the place within which the teachings are transmitted.

The wisdom that has no teacher is contained within each and every one of us. It is made of the same stuff that the universe itself is made of. When our self and the universe—two seemingly different realms—are in resonance with each other, the illusory gap closes. Then we begin to recognize that all things, including ourselves, are constantly expressing the inherent perfection that exists as the universe. And we see that even within the apparent chaos and confusion, there is something that is constantly nourishing, directly pointing to the ways in which we can awaken to the truth that is already there.

To live this life means to be willing to embark on a journey of discovery. Dogen says, "How can ordinary thinking completely comprehend that the power of the teachings touches the body and mind?" We must throw away our ordinary thinking and be willing to enter the unknown. The truth is always realized within each one of us. And the need to know this truth is the beating heart of spiritual practice. By uncovering what has always been there, it makes visible the invisible.

If you're not intimate with it,
when it's revealed,
you'll think about it for the rest of your life.
When words and ideas are finally obliterated,
the light first appears.
Light or no light,
wet with the morning dew,
the tips of ten thousand grasses.

*Those without minds and without bodies
        can obtain benefit from
hearing the teachings.*

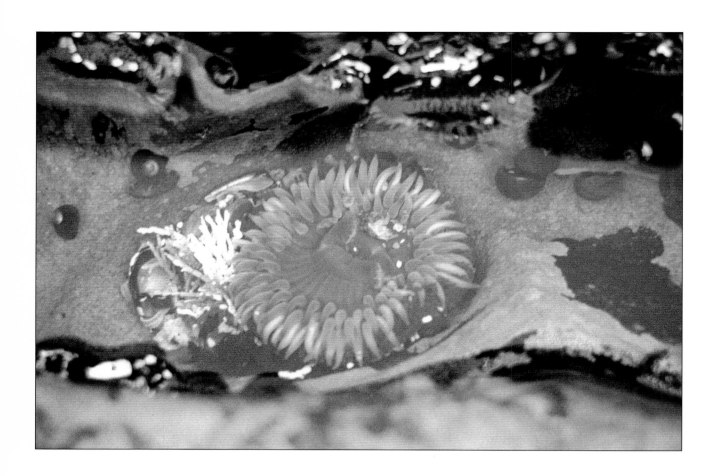

Whenever the merit and virtue of hearing the teachings are planted in the field of the mind and body, they never wither. Hearing the teachings inevitably matures and bears fruit. Foolish people think that if they do not advance on the path of understanding and cannot remember the teachings even though they hear them constantly, then there is no merit. They think they must listen frequently to learning and writings with their whole mind and body. They think, "What benefit can there be if I forget the talk while still on my seat and feel uncertain as I get up? What educational merit could there be?" They think like this because they have not encountered, or even seen, an authentic teacher. An authentic teacher is someone who has received the authentic transmission face-to-face. An authentic teacher is someone to whom the realized ones have truly transmitted. When foolish people say they are conscious of some teachings and remember them for a short time, those are the times when the efficacy of hearing the teachings, even if they are only slightly aware of it, envelops the mind and envelops consciousness.

Commentary 13

In his opening statement to this section, Dogen touches on a pivotal matter that comes into play when we try to really hear the teachings of the insentient. There are three key concepts here that we should investigate thoroughly. They are "hearing," "planted," and "never wither." "Hearing" means standing on the ground, facing the teachings. To "stand on the ground" is to have raised in one's consciousness the aspiration to realize the truth of the universe. To "face the teachings" is to have established a body and mind that are open and receptive—a place for the teachings to enter. When this happens, the teachings are "planted in the field of mind and body." That is, they take root.

But we should understand that the roots are already present. They have not grown from the outside. The teachings are already present and have not entered from an outer source. It is just simply that when one stands on the ground and faces the teachings, what is created is a fertile moment of unfolding. That the teachings never wither is implicit in the fact that they have always been present. They are present before they're acknowledged, while they're being acknowledged, after they have been acknowledged, and even if they are never acknowledged. When this acknowledgement *does* take place, maturation and the bearing of fruit naturally follow. This truth may or may not be realized. Nonetheless, maturation and the bearing of fruit naturally follow.

Our natural tendency is to want to know. We frantically grasp at certainty. However, the realm that Dogen speaks of is beyond knowing and certainty. It is essentially ungraspable. If we do manage to grasp some part of it and turn it in our mind, we may be able to produce a kind of tangible expression of our experience. But that is no longer the immediate experience. There is the sweet fragrance and gentle touch of a spring breeze. But when we try to capture it, put it in a jar and label it "spring breeze," it is no longer the experience. We should appreciate, however, that it is possible for a skilled artist—through the use of imagery, music, or poetry—to invoke the experience of the spring breeze without naming it, analyzing it or categorizing it. This kind of expression just allows the experience to be present. It enters the consciousness of the audience and awakens in them the reality of the spring breeze. These events are not encountered on the path of understanding. They only reveal themselves along the path of trust, openness and receptivity.

Dogen speaks of the authentic teacher as someone to whom the realized ones have truly transmitted. This transmission is generally understood to be the transmission of the truth from one generation to the next. However, to be truly transmitted to goes far beyond this ordinary transmission. It is the holding of the wisdom of countless generations of realized ones as one's own body and mind. And yet, there is no conscious awareness of this holding. There are no teachings to be remembered. There is no information to be processed. There is no learning to be had. The teachings just subtly envelop the mind and envelop consciousness.

Inconceivably wondrous is this reality.
Exquisitely all-pervading is this truth.

It has nothing to do with cosmic consciousness or the divine self. It exists in life and death, prior to life and death, and after life and death. Before there ever was movement and stillness, sound and silence, being and nonbeing, there has always been this truth. It is not to be found in metaphors, images or thoughts. Indeed, it's not like anything. Do not be deluded. It is nothing other than what you do morning and night.

Bright day, blue sky
> *in a dream*
> *explaining a dream.*

Whenever the merit and virtue
        of hearing the teachings are planted
in the field of the mind and body,
        they never wither.

Exactly at authentic moments like these, there are the merits and virtues of enveloping the body, enveloping what is before the body, enveloping the mind, enveloping what is before the mind, enveloping what is after the mind, enveloping causes, results, actions, conditions, natures, forms, power, enveloping the Buddha, enveloping the ancestors, enveloping self and other, enveloping skin, flesh, bones, and marrow, and so forth. By actualizing the merits and virtues of enveloping words and expression and enveloping sitting and lying down, they reach everywhere, from the smallest waves to the sky.

Truly it is hard to know the merit and virtue of this kind of hearing of the teachings. Nonetheless, if you meet in the great assembly of realized ones, and investigate the skin, flesh, bones, and marrow, you will ceaselessly draw the merit and power of the expressing of the teachings and there will be no place that you do not envelop with the spiritual power of hearing the teachings. Practicing in this way, whether the waves of the eons are slow or fast, you will eventually see the actualization of results. Although we should not irrationally throw out frequently listening to learning and writings, neither should we take this single aspect as an essential point. Those who study know this. Dongshan embodied this fully.

Commentary 14

Since it has existed before the beginning of time,
it cannot be attained.
Since it transcends time and space,
it is always in the eternal present.

What is "exactly at authentic moments like these"? What kind of moment can embrace all of these merits and virtues that Dogen describes? What is the place of the moment in the spectrum of time? It arrives and it leaves simultaneously. What does it contain? Indeed, does it even exist?

An ancient wise one once said, "If you want to understand the past, look at the present. If you want to understand the future, look at the present. Past, present and future are a single reality." That single reality exists "exactly at authentic moments like these." The "click" of a camera's shutter at 1/250 of a second, a flash of lightning in a summer sky, the blink of an eye—all are moments that contain the totality of time.

The simple process of taking the backward step and finding the still point within each one of us provides an opportunity to open up a space for the moment to come alive. Once we are able to bring our bodies to a point of rest, we are in a position to watch the flow of thoughts that race through our consciousness continuously, blotting out any possibility of being touched by the moment. But as our awareness simply watches the thoughts, by virtue of just that awareness itself, the thoughts slowly begin to diminish, and ultimately disappear. Again, when the thoughts disappear, the thinker disappears. When the thinker disappears, we come home to the moment, to the place where our life is taking place.

Certain effort and meticulousness are required in genuine spiritual practice. They are necessary if we are to truly embody and actualize the truth. Once the wisdom of the teachings of the insentient is fully absorbed, it unknowingly begins to manifest in everything that we do. It shows in our encounters and relationships, and in the way we understand ourselves and the universe. And yet there is no deliberate effort or self-consciousness in applying this wisdom to all of our activities. It functions because it is present in the body and in the mind.

The process of enabling this kind of spiritual unfolding is sometimes referred to as "the nurturing of the sacred fetus." It is a period of time after one has deeply realized and assimilated the teachings. At this point, the nurturing begins. All deliberate forms vanish. All traces of practice, of training, of realization dissolve and the ordinariness of life emerges. That is the most profound teaching of reality, and it is manifested in every action. The Way expresses itself as the Way.

At the beginning of the spiritual journey, mountains are mountains and rivers are rivers. Then after much study and reflection and going very deeply into oneself, one realizes that mountains are many things, and rivers are many things. They reach everywhere, encompassing the whole universe. And then, many years later, mountains are mountains and rivers are rivers.

There is an ancient collection of brush paintings called *The Ten Ox-herding Pictures*: ten illustrations depicting the journey of a spiritual practitioner from first entry into the spiritual path, to the culmination of the journey. The first painting shows a very young, almost childlike figure embarking on a search for the truth. The final painting shows an old person emerging from the mountains. Ragged of clothes, covered with dust, a joyful expression on the face, gleaming eyes reach out and engage you. A captivating smile disarms you. There is no air of enlightenment present. Indeed, you are not sure if you are looking at a sage or a fool. This is the physical manifestation of the myriad forms of the awakened ones appearing in infinite ways, appropriate to circumstances.

Entering the marketplace, barefoot and
*   unadorned.*
Blissfully smiling, though covered with dust
*   and ragged of clothes.*
Using no supernatural power, you bring
the withered trees spontaneously to bloom.

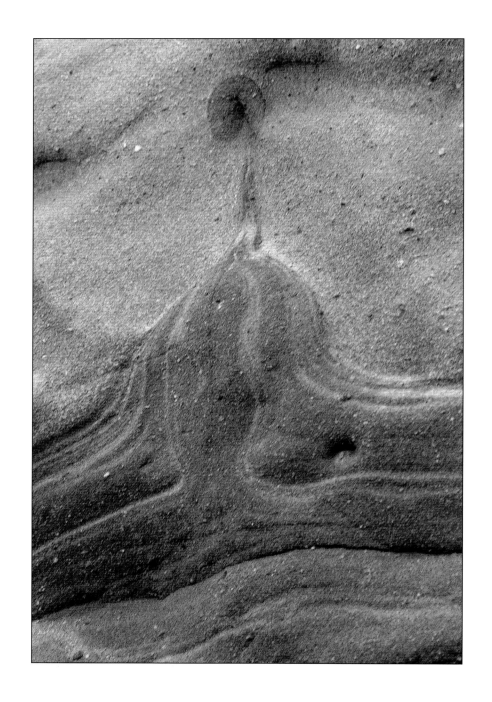

Truly, it is hard to know
the merit and virtue
of this kind of hearing of the teachings.

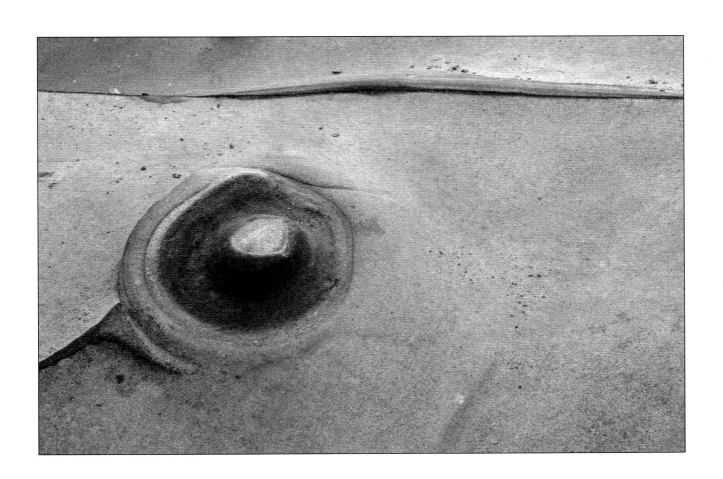

Yunyan said, "I am expressing it and still you do not hear. How much less likely that you will hear the insentient expressing the Way." In response to this actualization of the enlightenment of Dongshan, which immediately went beyond enlightenment, verifying even the vow of enlightenment, Yunyan opened his heart to Dongshan, thus sealing and verifying the bones and marrow of the ancestors. "You still do not hear when I express it." His is not the everyday meaning of these words. He is verifying and clarifying that the insentient expressing the Way, even if it has ten thousand aspects, is not the object of thinking. The continuation of the lineage on this occasion is what is key. Neither ordinary people nor the holy ones can easily reach and inquire into this.

Dongshan then composed a verse and offered it to Yunyan, saying, "The mystery of the insentient expressing the Way is so extraordinary, so extraordinary!" Both the insentient and the insentient expressing the Way are hard to conceptualize. What sort of thing is this "insentient" that he speaks about? You should study how it is neither ordinary nor holy, sentient nor insentient. The ordinary, the holy, the sentient, the insentient, together with expressing and not expressing—all belong to the realm of the conceptual.

Commentary 15

Opened up,
the ground of being ceaselessly meets itself.
If you take it conceptually,
you will miss it by ten thousand miles.

When Yunyan said, "I am expressing it and still you do not hear. How much less likely that you will hear the insentient expressing the Way," Dogen calls this a "response to the actualization of the enlightenment of Dongshan." Yunyan was verifying that Dongshan had not only realized the teachings of the insentient, but was also, in fact, actualizing them at that very moment. Do you understand? When the insentient speak, they speak insentient, and only the insentient can hear it. Ordinary beings cannot. Dongshan's actualization was present in his inability to hear his teacher's explanation. He had become deaf, dumb and blind, thus merging with the universe.

The sky is mute, yet the four seasons in all their beauty and diversity unfold there. The earth is deaf, dumb and blind, yet the ten thousand things are born here. What sense is there in describing reality when it can be experienced directly? When you finally cut off attachments and conceptual thinking, only then will you become free and unhindered.

Seeing that his student had left him, Yunyan opened his heart to Dongshan and certified his realization with the bones and marrow of the ancestors. He confirmed that Dongshan had actualized enlightenment beyond enlightenment. This kind of transmission is truly subtle, as well as critical in the movement of the realization of the truth from generation to generation. Even sages cannot easily grasp it.

"You still do not hear when I express it" is ordinary language, but the content of this phrase goes far beyond the ordinary and the holy. Yunyan is acknowledging something that cannot be expressed in everyday language. It cannot be held in a discriminating consciousness. He is verifying and clarifying that the insentient expressing the Way is not the consequence of linear thought.

Dongshan then composed a verse and offered it to his teacher:

The mystery of the insentient expressing the Way
is so extraordinary, so extraordinary!
Both the insentient and the insentient expressing
the Way are hard to conceptualize.

This is communication that does not take place between subject and object, *because* the insentient are neither ordinary nor holy, neither sentient nor insentient. Dogen relegates ordinary, holy, sentient and insentient—together with expressing or not expressing—to the realm of the conceptual. This is the realm of duality. It is also the realm of delusion, separation, confusion and suffering. There is a reality that transcends all dualities. But it is still a one-sided view of the universe. The truth is not to be found in unity or in differentiation. We must look for it in the meeting place of nonduality. Dongshan articulated his understanding of this meeting place after he left Yunyan. He was crossing a river, and upon seeing his reflection in the water while crossing a river, he said in verse:

Don't seek it from others
or you'll estrange from yourself.
I now go out alone—
everywhere I encounter it.
It is now me, yet I am not it.
One must understand it in this way
to merge with suchness.

Dongshan was essentially saying, "You and I are the same thing, yet I am not you and you are not me." Both of these facts exist simultaneously. He encountered this truth everywhere, and knew that it didn't come from others. It was embodied in his own being.

Dongshan's merging with suchness is the point of two arrows meeting in mid-air. It is the seal of the skin, flesh, bones, and marrow of an endless stream of wise ones and sages who have also tread this very ground—the ground of being—and who have also heard with the eye the voice of the insentient. Although this wondrous mystery may be realized and actualized by only a few, we must remember that all beings contain the inherent potential to awaken to the very voice that opened Dongshan's heart.

The mystery of the insentient
        expressing the Way
is so extraordinary, so extraordinary!

The insentient, right now, is mysterious and wondrous and yet again wondrous. It goes beyond the knowledge and consciousness of ordinary people and wise holy ones. It is not connected to the calculations of heavenly beings or humans.

"If you listen with the ears, it is incomprehensible." Even if you had heavenly ears, even if you had ears of the Way that span worlds and span time, when you try listening with the ears it is incomprehensible. Even if you had ears on top of a wall or ears on the head of a stick, you would not understand the insentient expressing the Way. That's because it is not a physical sound. It is not that there is no listening with the ears, but even if you exhausted 100,000 eons of effort, it would be incomprehensible. The insentient expressing the Way is a direct way of being, which is apart from sounds and forms; it is not a nest or cave in the realm of the ordinary or the holy.

"If you hear sounds with the eyes, it is truly knowable." Nowadays people think that hearing sounds with the eyes refers to the coming and going of grasses, trees, blossoms, or birds, which are seen with the eyes. This idea is mistaken, and is not at all the Buddha's teaching.

Commentary 16

The sky is clear and the sun appears;
rain falls and the earth is moistened.
Everything is clear as it is,
yet how few are really able to see it.

The way the insentient expound the teachings is not through a physical sound. It does not rely on the conventional passage of sound waves through the air. It is, rather, intimate expression, a kind of communication that is not apparent to the senses, or to the intellect. It is direct, immediate and complete experience, where two apparently different entities are actually functioning as a single object—that is, they are completely identified.

In the Japanese language, there is the word *mitsu* which means "secret" or "esoteric." It is that which is not apparent to the senses or intellect. It implies a direct, immediate, and complete experience with no separation, like two things that are actually the same. The other part of the word, *go*, means "words," so *mitsugo* means "secret talk,"—speech that is communicated directly without sound. This is intimate communication. Yet we don't need to see it as particularly mystical. Direct, intuitive perception is an ability that all beings have. When Dogen speaks of *mitsugo*, he explains that it is a state of direct contact with reality which is secret only in the sense that it is beyond explanation. He is not referring to some kind of esoteric teaching. Even within the world of experimental physics, this kind of communication has been demonstrated.

In an experiment carried out in Geneva, Switzerland, scientists took pairs of photons and sent them along optical fibers in opposite directions to sensors in two villages north and south of Geneva. Reaching the ends of the fibers, the photons were forced to make a random choice between two alternative and equally possible pathways. Since there is no obvious way for the photons to communicate with each other, classical physics predicts that one photon's choice of a path will have no relationship or effect on the other's. But when the results were studied, the "independent" decisions made by the pair of photons always matched and complemented each other exactly, even though there was no physical way for them to relay information back and forth. If there had been communication, it would have had to exceed the speed of light—which, according to the work of Einstein, is not possible. Clearly, in this experiment information was not being transferred from one place to another. And yet, each photon responded in a way that mirrored its distant twin's response. The connection and correlation between the two particles were instantaneous. They were behaving as if they were a single reality.

Intimate speech is beyond space and time. It has nothing to do with geographical or temporal distances. It is outside the passage of time. In it, "no communication whatsoever is possible." The reason this is true is that apparently separate entities are in fact a single reality. The insentient speak to the insentient. The insentient hear the insentient.

Our minds are wonderful instruments. At this point in the history of our species, we have yet to exhaust our human potential. Even great minds have barely scratched its surface. Analytical thinking has allowed us to create many of the wonderful technological advances and medical cures. But it has also created unimaginable horrors and destruction.

In that aspect of our consciousness that is intuitive and direct, the mind functions in an instant, like a flash of lightning. It is this facet of human consciousness that is barely recognized or developed in our educational system and culture. What kind of world would this be if we were able to function beyond the dualities, beyond linear, sequential thought? What would happen if we could enter into real intimacy with one another—indeed, with the whole universe?

The insentient expressing the Way
is not a nest or cave
in the realm of the ordinary or the holy.

In studying Dongshan's "hear sounds with the eye," it is the eye where one hears the sound of the insentient expressing the Way. It is the eye where one manifests the sound of the insentient expressing the Way. You should study this eye extensively. Because the eye's hearing sound ought to be the same as the ear's hearing sound, the eye's hearing sound is not the same as the ear's hearing sound. Do not study with the idea that there is an ear faculty within the eye. Do not study with the idea that the eye is identical to the ear. Do not study with the idea that sound is manifest behind the eye.

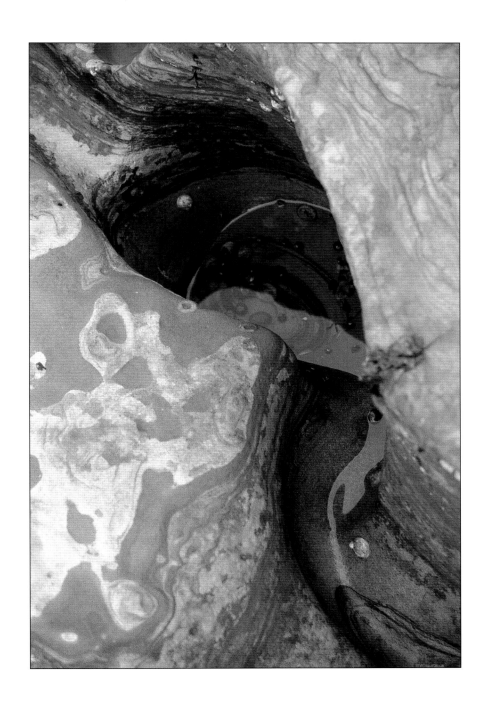

Commentary 17

Look! the bright shining sun lights up the sky.
Listen! the pure whispering wind
circles this great earth. Enter here.

The eye that hears sounds is the mystic eye, the eye that is capable of penetrating beyond the surface of things, into what is not so apparent. It is the eye that hears and manifests the teachings of the insentient. Dogen encourages us to study this eye extensively. What does it mean to really see with the mystic eye? What does it mean to enter the realm of true seeing? What does it mean to see beyond superficial appearances and to perceive a whole other aspect of existence that is hidden from view?

An ancient Zen master said, "The eye that grasps the universe is so perceptive that it does not miss even a single thread." When this mystic eye functions, it goes beyond looking and enters the realm of seeing and hearing in a very different way. Looking speaks to what things are. Seeing reveals what else things are—the hidden aspect of the full reality of a rock, tree, a mountain, a dog or a person. Walt Whitman said, "You must not know too much or be too precise or scientific about birds and trees and flowers and water... a certain free margin, and even vagueness—perhaps ignorance, credulity—helps you in your enjoyment of these things."

Evelyn Underhill, in her classic book *Mysticism*, writes extensively about the mystic's education in seeing and hearing. She says:

The education which tradition has ever prescribed for the mystic consists in the gradual development of an extraordinary faculty of concentration, a power of spiritual attention. It's not enough that she should naturally be aware of the absolute, unless she be able to contemplate it... The condition of all valid seeing and hearing upon every plane of consciousness lies not in the sharpening of the senses, but in a particular attitude of the whole personality: in a self-forgetting attentiveness, a profound concentration or self-merging, which operates a real communion between seer and seen—in a word, contemplation.

She clarifies that this "communion" applies not only to what she calls "divine reality," but to all aspects of our life. "It's a mental attitude under which all things give up to us the secret of their life."

In the realm of communication that Dongshan experienced and that Dogen speaks of, there exists a resonance, a recognition of a link between subject and object that manifests as energy that streams back and forth between the two. The barrier between its life and your own melts away as you are merged with it through an act of communion. And yet, what is heard and what is seen—although it is understood intimately—remains essentially inexpressible. Heart speaks to heart, life to life, but not to our surface consciousness. All that surface consciousness knows is that a communication was received, and that it was true and wondrous. This is how the teachings of the insentient are communicated. This is how the 84,000 gates, the limitless gates, are opened.

We think that the sound we hear with the eye ought to be the same as the ear's hearing of sound, but it's not. The eye and the ear are not identical. There are myriad dimensions to hearing. Some can be heard by the ear. Others can only be heard by the eye.

In the depths of stillness all words melt away.
Clouds disperse and it miraculously manifests
      before you.
When seen, it is filled with wonder,
      vast and without edges, nothing concealed.

In the depths of stillness all words melt away, clouds disperse and it miraculously manifests before you. Clouds disperse and it vividly appears before you. "It" appears. It cannot be summoned. It cannot be demanded. It cannot be conjured. It will appear when you are ready to see it. *When seen, it is filled with wonder, vast and without edges, nothing is concealed.* Another master presents it in this way:

Silently and serenely one forgets all words. Clearly and vividly, it appears before you. When one realizes it, it is vast and without edges. In its essence one is clearly aware. Singularly reflecting is this bright awareness, full of wonder is this pure reflection. Dew and the moon, stars and streams, snow on pine trees, and clouds hovering on the mountain peaks. From darkness, they all become glowingly bright. From obscurity they all turn to resplendent light.

Dogen's appreciation of that mystical dimension of the world around him is beautifully expressed in this passage: "Trees and rocks flourish and abound, and the birds and the beasts take on a supernatural excellence." It is important to see that supernatural excellence for ourselves. How do we appreciate it? We should ask ourselves this question every day.

It is the eye where one hears
the sound of the insentient
expressing the Way.

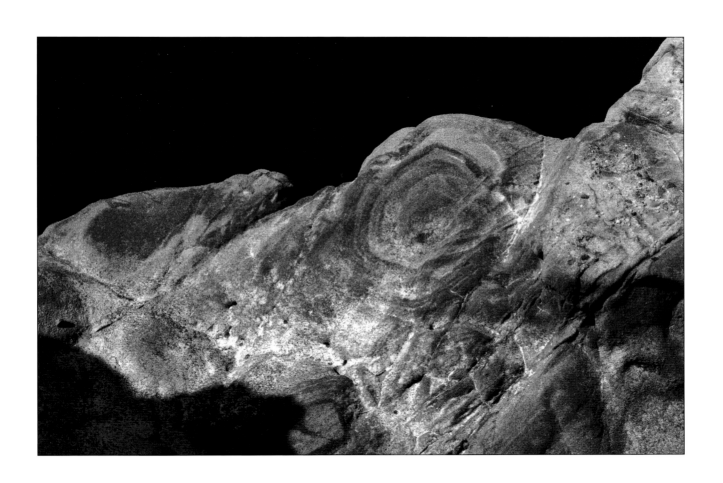

An ancient said, "All the worlds in the ten directions are a monastic's single eye." Do not compare these teachings and conclude that if one were to hear sounds with this single eye, it would be the same as Dongshan's teaching of "hearing sounds with the eyes." Even though we study the ancient's words, "all the worlds in the ten directions," and "a single eye," all ten directions are just this single eye. Moreover, there is the eye of a thousand hands. There is the eye of the true teachings. There is the eye of a thousand ears. There is the eye of a thousand tongues. There is the eye of a thousand minds. There is the eye of a thousand realized minds. There is the eye of a thousand realized bodies. There is the eye of a thousand staffs. There is the eye of a thousand precursors of the body. There is the eye of a thousand precursors of the mind. There is the eye of a thousand deaths in death. There is the eye of a thousand lives in life. There is the eye of a thousand selves. There is the eye of a thousand others. There is the eye of a thousand eyes. There is the eye of a thousand studies. There is the eye of a thousand verticals. There is the eye of a thousand horizontals.

Commentary 18

The river runs through it, never having wet it.
The spring breeze passes through it, never having entered.
There is no place to put the great heart of compassion.

"All the worlds in the ten directions are a monastic's single eye." Since this eye is all the worlds in the ten directions, can there be any doubt that it must belong to all beings—sentient and insentient alike? The ten directions is all directions. It includes everything. So, if that eye encompasses the whole universe in the ten directions, it is, of necessity, everyone's eye. It is the whole body of each and every one of us.

The full quote that Dogen is referring to reads, *All the worlds in the ten directions are a monastic's single eye. The entire universe is the complete body of a monastic. The entire universe is your own light. The entire universe is within your own luminosity. In the entire universe there is no one who is not your own self.* However, to study the eye in the ten directions is not yet the embodiment of the eye. What is the embodiment of the eye as one's own body, as one's activity in the world, as one's own self?

In general, hearing the teachings of the Way is not just a matter of physical hearing or conscious hearing. It is hearing the teachings with all force, all mind, all body, all speech, from as far in the past as before your father and mother were born, before the first sound in the universe, up to the limit of the future and the unlimited future beyond that. It is hearing the teachings before the body and after the mind.

Yet all of these innumerable ways of hearing are still not the same as Dongshan's "hearing sounds with the eye."

Dogen tells us that Yunyan's lifeblood intermingled with Dongshan's, and a new generation was born. Generation after generation, down to the present time, this is the way that the ability to hear the teachings of the insentient has been awakened. This teaching is mysterious and wondrous. It is beyond the knowledge and consciousness of ordinary people *and* sages. Dogen says, "If you listen with the ears, it is incomprehensible. Even if you had heavenly ears, even if you had ears of the Way that span worlds and span time." It is not a physical sound, and yet it's not that it doesn't exist. It *does* exist, but it's difficult—if not impossible—to understand. This is because it doesn't come from the outside.

"Even if you had ears on top of a wall or ears on the head of a stick, you would not understand the insentient expressing the Way." There once was a hermit who was blind. After a rain, on a muddy road, he would wear pure white shoes and go to the market. Someone once asked him, "You're blind. How come there's no mud on your shoes?" The mountain man raised his staff and said, "There's an eye on this staff." A master commented on this, "The mountain man is proof that when reaching for a pillow at night, there is an eye in the hand. When eating, there is an eye on the tongue. When recognizing people on hearing them speak, there is an eye in the ears."

Wisdom, the clarity of seeing the nature of the universe, and compassion, the manifestation of that clarity in one's actions, always go hand in hand. True insight into the nature of the universe is insight into the nature of the self. Once seen, it spontaneously manifests as a response to take care of that universe.

In Zen, compassion is frequently represented as the figure of Avalokiteshvara, the bodhisattva who postpones her enlightenment to remain in the world and assist all beings in putting an end to suffering. She has thousands of eyes to see the sources of pain, and manifold hands to take care of them. Because of her realization she is utterly blind. Because of her realization, each hand is endowed with a clear-seeing eye.

Avalokiteshvara always manifests herself in whatever form is appropriate to the circumstance. Sometimes she is a saint, sometimes a general, sometimes a derelict. Every time someone responds to an accident, every time a fireman enters a fire, every time a mother turns towards her crying child, Avalokiteshvara bodhisattva comes to life. There are many bodhisattvas, beings who put aside their realization, their own enlightenment,

for the benefit of others. Not until every single sentient being on the face of this earth is enlightened do the bodhisattvas take care of their own enlightenment. There are bodhisattvas in all religions and in each one we find this great compassionate heart at work. But what is that great compassionate heart?

Wisdom is the realization of no separation. Compassion is the actualization of wisdom and its activity in the world. In compassion there is no sense of a doer or doing. It happens. If someone falls, you pick them up. If there's a cry, you respond. A master said:

A thousand hands illustrate the many-sidedness of the guidance...in the salvation of beings. A thousand eyes illustrate the breadth of emanating light to illuminate the darkness. If there were no sentient beings and no mundane turmoil, then not even a finger would remain, much less thousands or tens of thousands of arms. Not even an eyelid would be there, much less thousands or tens of thousands of eyes.

It's because of delusion that there's enlightenment. It's because of enlightenment that there's delusion. Because there is suffering, there are the ten thousand hands and eyes of great compassion. But where do they come from? How do they function? How can they be awakened? What shape is the spring? What color is it? *What* is it? We can't really say. Nevertheless, it is able to accord with things and to come in its time, unhindered. There is no stopping spring. When it arrives, it truly arrives— so too does the great heart of compassion.

All the worlds in the ten directions
are a monastic's single eye.

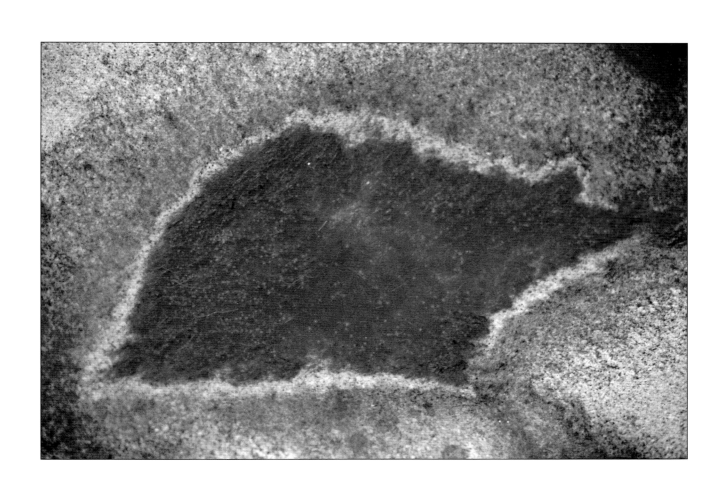

Therefore, if you study all eyes as all worlds, still you do not investigate deeply into the eye. Just make an urgent effort to investigate, by means of your eye, hearing the insentient expressing the Way. Now, the point of Dongshan's teaching is that it is hard for the ear to understand the insentient expressing the Way. The eye hears sounds. Moreover, there is hearing sounds with the realized body. There is hearing sounds with the all-pervasive body. Even if you do not investigate the eye hearing sounds, you should physically attain "the insentient can hear the insentient express the Way." You should drop away body and mind.

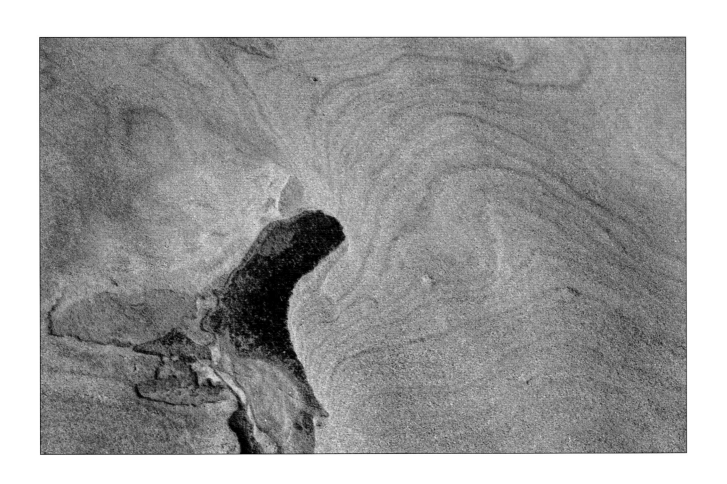

Commentary 19

*When the heavens collapse
and the earth disintegrates,
the inconceivable, clear, bright mind
is not destroyed.*

If we are to understand Dongshan's teaching about hearing with the eye, we must first examine hearing with the realized body, hearing with the all-pervasive body, and physically attaining the insentient hearing the insentient expressing the Way. Are these three different things, or are they three different ways of perceiving the same thing?

Dongshan, the National Teacher, Yunyan, and Dogen, throughout their teachings speak from the perspective of nonduality, in which everything interpenetrates with everything else in identity and interdependence, in causality and origination. They're describing a universe in which everything needs everything else, and in which there's not a single speck of dust that does not affect the whole. It is in this realm that the insentient hear the insentient expressing the Way. This way of understanding ourselves and the universe is not just a philosophical postulation; it's a description of the realized truth of the universe. Mountains, rivers, the great earth and the self—where are the distinctions to be found? Why is this all divided into twos and threes? How do the complications arise? Indeed, what is it that you are calling your self?

What is the realized body? To realize means to make real that which is, to become aware of something that already exists. What is it to realize the truth of the body? Is it this bag of skin within which we find ourselves? Or is there more to it?

Dogen also speaks of "hearing sounds with the all-pervasive body"—the everywhere-body. What is this? We say that it reaches everywhere. How does it reach everywhere? In actual fact, it's not so much a matter of "how," but rather, a matter of "is." *It reaches everywhere.* It's the truth of our existence. We just need to discover it. "How" implies the need for some kind of explanation or knowledge. That's not the all-pervasive body. That's not the interdependent universe.

This image of a completely unified universe can be found in an ancient scripture called the *Flower Garland Sutra*. In it is contained a teaching called the diamond net of Indra, wherein all existence is seen as a vast net of diamonds that extends throughout the universe—not only in the three dimensions of space, but in the fourth dimension of time as well. It describes the all-pervasive body; it describes the truth of our life.

The net of Indra is a huge net of multifaceted diamonds in which each diamond reflects every other diamond, and as such, contains them. Every single diamond is both a unique entity and an integral part of the whole. And although this diamond net is only a metaphor, it is the expression of an experience that has been verified again and again for thousands of years through the lives of the men and women who have practiced the Way. It describes how each and every thing contains every other thing.

This description of the universe would have remained an obscure religious experience, were it not for some remarkable discoveries that emerged in the mid-twentieth century. It was found that if a photograph is made of a three-dimensional subject illuminated by laser light—an audience, for example—a piece of film containing an interference pattern is created. When this film is illuminated again by laser light, a three-dimensional image of the object is projected, and a person can literally walk into it. This three-dimensional image is the hologram. As remarkable as this discovery is, more intriguing is the fact that if you cut the piece of film in half and project light through half of it, you would still get the whole image— nothing is lost. Cutting each half in half down to the smallest fragment, produces the same result. No one is left out of the projection. Every single bit of information contained in the full piece of film is contained in its smallest fragment. Each diamond contains every other diamond.

Similarly, it has been found that our senses are sensitive to a much broader range of frequencies than was previously suspected. Research has shown for instance, that our visual systems are sensitive to sound, and that even the cells in our bodies are sensitive to a broad range of frequencies. In other words, we perceive "with the whole body and mind." It is only in the holographic domain of consciousness—the brain—that such frequencies are sorted and divided up into conventional perceptions such as hearing, sight, taste, and the like. We take these frequencies and we create what we call reality. The three worlds are nothing but mind.

The three worlds, mind, and things
are without separation.
Therefore, how can it be spoken of
or understood?

There is hearing sounds with the realized body.
      There is hearing sounds with the all-pervasive body.

Because this teaching was passed on, my late teacher Jujing, the old Buddha, said, "The gourd vine entangles the gourd." This is "expressing the Way," and the "insentient," through which the true eye of Dongshan has been passed on, through which the bones and marrow of Dongshan have been passed on. Due to the teaching that everything that expresses the Way is insentient, this is the insentient expressing the Way, and is what is called a "textual precedent." The insentient is that which expresses the Way for the sake of the insentient. What is it that is called "insentient"? You should know. It is that which listens to the insentient expressing the Way. What is it that is called "expressing the Way"? You should know. It is that which does not know that it is itself insentient.

A monastic once asked Great Master Touzi, "What is 'the insentient expressing the Way'?" The Master said, "Don't speak ill." Now, what Master Touzi teaches is surely the spiritual charter of the ancient realized ones, the governing edict of the lineage of ancestors. Both "the insentient express the Way" and "that which expresses the Way is insentient" are not speaking ill. You should know this. "The insentient expressing the Way" is the complete text of the realized ones and ancestors. The followers of Linji and Deshan do not know it. Only one-by-one do the realized ones and ancestors investigate it, realize it, and actualize it.

Commentary 20

Each and every thing, all real;
each and every one, all complete.
Where attainment and knowing cannot reach,
there it stands alone.

Dogen says that because the teaching was passed on, his own teacher said, "The gourd vine entangles the gourd." "Vines and entanglements" is a phrase used in Asian philosophy to describe difficulties or complications. The difficulty resides in the impossibility of adequately expressing with words the nature of the truth. Dogen's teacher's saying, "The gourd vine entangles the gourd" describes bottled gourd vines intertwining with other bottle gourd vines. This is a poetic metaphor for mind being transmitted by mind. Indeed, it can be said that the bottled gourd is nothing other than vines and entanglements. This is the expression of the Way and the teachings of the insentient that were passed from Yunyan to Dongshan. This is also the true eye realized by Dongshan, passed on to future generations.

Dogen describes this expression as "the bones and marrow of Dongshan" being passed on. "Bones and marrow" is a reference to the totality of being that moves from generation to generation when the teaching is fully realized and fully embodied. Each generation hears—and already has—the bones and marrow. In other words, Dogen is once again emphasizing that the transmission does not happen through the acquisition of knowledge or understanding, but through an awakening. It is an acknowledgement of the presence of the bones and marrow of that teaching as being already in one's own body and mind. Because of this inherent wisdom, everything that expresses the Way is insentient. And this, in and of itself, is the insentient expressing the Way. Further, we should remember that the insentient is that which expresses the Way solely for the sake of the insentient.

Dogen then says that what is called insentient is "that which listens to the insentient expressing the Way." He also says that the insentient "is that which does not know that it is itself insentient." Not knowing can only be present within the realm of intimacy. In not knowing, the reference system drops away. The dualistic way of perceiving the universe or oneself no longer exists. This is the intimacy of seeing form and hearing sounds with the whole body and mind. It's not that it cannot be experienced; it's just that it remains ineffable. It is ultimately the gourd vine entangling the gourd.

Dizang asked Fayan, "Where are you going?"
Fayan said, "I'm wandering on a pilgrimage."
Dizang said, "What is the purpose of your pilgrimage?"
Fayan said, "I don't know."
Dizang, "Ah! Not knowing…very intimate; very intimate indeed."

Although not knowing is very intimate, we may ask, of what use is it? Once we reach that intimate place of not knowing, what then? It doesn't function. On the other hand, it's clear that knowing is illusory. Going to the words and ideas, we inevitably end up entangled in a forest of brambles. Ultimately, the Way is not to be found in either knowing or not knowing. Knowing is false consciousness. Not knowing is indifference. This being the case, how are we to proceed?

As for Master Touzi's "Do not speak ill," this is a warning not to fall into the deep pit of intellectualization and rationalization. Thinking only creates barriers that ultimately hinder the sense of intimacy required to truly hear the insentient expressing the Way. Dogen reminds us that both "the insentient express the Way" and "that which expresses the Way is insentient," are not speaking ill. We should realize that these phrases do not fall into the trap of explanations, but rather, awaken the possibility of discovery that goes beyond knowing and not knowing.

Fools and sages all live in its presence.
Move toward it, and the sickness is increased.
Describe it, and you miss its reality.

It is this Way—the Way that goes beyond knowing and not knowing—that all of the sages and realized ones have been able to investigate, realize and actualize for thousands of years. It is the wonder of the experience of the insentient expressing the truth of the universe.

What is it that is called "expressing the Way"?
  It is that which does not know
that it is itself insentient.

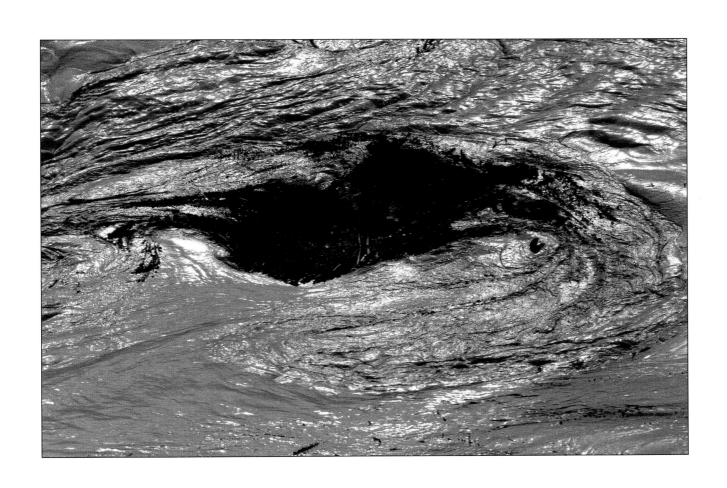

About the Photographs

Using photographs to illustrate the commentary on Master Dogen's "Teachings of the Insentient" follows a precedent established in 1978. At the time I was working with my teacher Taizan Maezumi Roshi on the book *The Way of Everyday Life*, using photographs as visual capping phrases—verses used in Zen to reveal and complement the essential point or heart of a koan. In this book, three capping images visually summarize the essence of the teaching contained in each section.

All of the photographs were taken on a single day, October 26, 1999, at Point Lobos, California with Fujichrome Provia 400F Professional film. A Nikon Camera equipped with medium focal length lenses was used to make the exposures. The film was then custom processed into the transparencies used to produce this book.

backward step turning one's attention inward; studying the self through Zen meditation and practice.

Bodhidharma an Indian monk known for taking Buddhism from India to China and later Japan, where he settled at Shaolin monastery and practiced meditation for nine years facing the wall.

buddha nature according to Mahayana Buddhism, the true, enlightened and immutable nature of all beings.

Caodong School *(J. Soto)* one of the Five Schools of Chinese Zen, founded by Dongshan Lianjie and Caoshan Benji in the ninth century; it was revitalized and brought to Japan by Eihei Dogen.

Caoxi stream southeast of Shaochou Kwantung. The waves of Caoxi refers to the teaching of the Sixth Ancestor of Zen, Huineng.

daruma school school of Zen Buddhism founded by Dainichi Nonin in 1189; its emphasis was on insight as taught by the Chinese Master Dahui.

demon's cave realm of delusion.

Deshan *(J. Tokusan, 780-865, C.E.),* a successor of Longtan, he taught at Mt. De.

Dongshan *(J. Tozan, 807-869, C.E.),* a Successor of Yunyan, he was the author of the "Song of Bright Mirror Samadhi." Together with Caoshan, he is regarded as the founder of the Caodong School, one of the five schools of Chinese Zen.

enlightenment the direct experience of one's true nature.

face-to-face teaching *(J. dokusan)* private interview with the teacher during which students present and clarify their understanding of the teachings.

falling away of body and mind state in which the mind is absorbed in intense concentration, free from distractions and goals; single-pointedness of mind.

Flower Garland Sutra Mahayana sutra that constitutes the basis of the Chinese Huayan *(J. Kegon)* school; it emphasizes mutually unobstructed interpenetration and states that Buddha, mind, and universe are identical to one another.

great Way the practice of realization taught by Shakyamuni Buddha; the nature of reality.

Guishan *(J. Issan, 771-853, C.E.)* a successor of Baizhang Huaihai, he taught at Mt. Gui. Guishan and his heir Yangshan are regarded as the co-founders of the Guiyang School, one of the five schools of Chinese Zen. He was also called Dagui (Great Gui).

heavenly beings divinities who inhabit the heavenly realm.

holding up a flower the first transmission of the teachings from Shakyamuni Buddha to Mahakashyapa; i.e., Shakyamuni held up a flower in front of an assembly of thousands, and only Mahakashyapa smiled and blinked his eyes.

hungry ghosts beings that suffer from greed and hunger, with their immense bellies and mouths as small as the eye of a needle.

insentient beings ordinarily not called "living," like mountains, rocks, and tiles, but which nevertheless have the ability to express the dharma.

kalpa a world cycle; an endlessly long period of time.

Jujing *(J. Tendo Nyojo, 1163-1228, C.E.)* Chinese Zen master of the Caodong School and successor of Zhenxie, as well as Dogen's teacher.

koan an apparently paradoxical statement or question used in Zen training to induce in students an intense level of doubt, allowing them to cut through conditioned descriptions of reality and see directly into their true nature.

Linji *(J. Rinzai ?-866, C.E.)* Chinese Zen master; successor of Huangbo and founder of the Rinzai school of Zen, one of the two schools of Buddhism still active in Japan.

mind-to-mind transmission confirmation of the merging of the minds of teacher and disciple; also the recognition of the buddha mind and entrustment of the teaching.

Mountains and Rivers Sutra a fascicle in the *Shobogenzo* depicting the interrelatedness of the absolute and the relative.

Mount Gridhrakuta Vulture Peak, the site of many of Shakyamuni Buddha's recorded discourses; site of the first transmission from the Buddha to Mahakashyapa.

Nanyang, National Teacher *(J. Nan'yo Echu, 675?-775?, C.E.)* successor of the Sixth Ancestor Huineng, and teacher to two emperors of Tang Dynasty China.

nirvana union with the absolute; in Zen it is essential to realize that samsara is nirvana, form is emptiness, that all beings are innately perfect from the outset.

nondual dharma essential principle of all existence; nondiscrimination or the lack of dualistic opposition.

Past Seven Buddhas buddhas who appeared in the world before the time of the historical Buddha, Shakyamuni.

practice also ceaseless practice; according to Master Dogen, a continuous process of actualizing enlightenment.

realization *see enlightenment.*

realized ones *see sages.*

sages advanced Zen practitioners; earlier awakened teachers of the dharma lineage.

sentient beings living beings, including humans; sometimes indicates those who are not awakened.

Shakyamuni Buddha Siddhartha Gautama, the historical Buddha and founder of Buddhism; he was a prince of the Shakya clan, living in northern India in the sixth century B.C.E.

skillful means forms that the teachings take, reflecting their appropriateness to the circumstances in which they appear.

skin, flesh, bones and marrow refers to the transmission of the teachings from Bodhidharma to each one of his four disciples, i.e. "You have obtained my skin; you have obtained my flesh…"

suchness *see thusness.*

sutra narrative text consisting chiefly of the discourses and teachings of the Buddha.

teachings dharma in Buddhism; universal truth or law; the Buddha's teachings; all phenomena that make up reality.

ten thousand things all phenomena.

Tiandai Buddhism school based on the Lotus Sutra and the teaching of the three truths: emptiness, temporal limitation of existence, and suchness.

Touzi *(J. Tosu, 819-914, C.E.)* successor of Cuiwei; he taught at Mt. Touzi.

thusness tathata; the absolute, true state of phenomena. It is immutable, immovable, and beyond all concepts and distinctions.

Yunyan *(J. Ungan, 782-841, C.E.)* sucessor of Yaoshan; he taught at Mt. Yunyan.

Zhaozhou *(J. Joshu, 778-897, C.E.)* one of the most important Zen masters of China during the Tang dynasty; dharma successor of Nanquan and greatly admired by Master Dogen; known for originating the koan "Mu."

About Zen Mountain Monastery and the Mountains and Rivers Order

Zen Mountain Monastery (ZMM), the main house of the Mountains and Rivers Order of Zen Buddhism, is a monastic center providing traditional yet distinctly American Zen training to people of all ages and religious backgrounds. Recognized as one of the leading Zen Buddhist monasteries in the West, it makes available year-round Zen training under the guidance of its founder and abbot, John Daido Loori, Roshi. With a resident community of female and male monastics and lay-trainees, ZMM offers a wide variety of programs and retreats related to Buddhism.

Located amid the scenic splendor of the mountains and rivers of the Catskill State Park, the Monastery's 230 acres nestle within the southern bowl of Tremper Mountain, bordered by the juncture of two of upstate New York's finest waterways, the Beaverkill and Esopus rivers. Designated by the Monastery's Board of Directors as a nature sanctuary to remain "forever wild," the property is also home to the Zen Environmental Studies Institute, a corporation offering education and training in Zen as it addresses our relationship with the environment.

The Society of Mountains and Rivers is an international umbrella organization for affiliates associated with the Monastery. A network of sitting groups in the United States and abroad provides facilities and visiting teachers, exploring projects that bring spiritual practice into every area of life.

Zen Center of New York City (also known as Fire Lotus Zendo) in the heart of Brooklyn is the New York City branch of ZMM, and a model for how a lay center can meet the needs of urban practitioners. Rapidly growing, it is directed by Bonnie Myotai Treace Sensei and senior staff. Lotus Flower Affiliate of Green Haven Correctional Facility provides an example of viable and powerful practice, with genuine Zen training flourishing behind the walls of this maximum security prison. The Monastery represents Buddhism on the advisory council to the governor on religions in the prisons, and Geoffrey Shugen Arnold, Sensei coordinates the National Buddhist Prison Sangha.

The Mountains and Rivers Order extends wide and sustained support to lay practitioners who maintain families and households. Dharma Communications is ZMM's educational outreach, and it provides the general public with audiovisual materials, electronic media and publications on Buddhism, arts, sciences, ethics, social action, business and ecology. Among John Daido Loori's books are: *Two Arrows Meeting in Mid-Air* (Dharma Communications Press, 2004), *The Art of Just Sitting* (Wisdom Publications, 2002), *Making Love with Light* (DC Press, 2000), *Teachings of the Insentient* (DC Press, 1999), *The Heart of Being* (Charles E. Tuttle Co., 1994), and *The Eight Gates of Zen* (DC Press, 1992). To order our books or to obtain more information about Zen Mountain Monastery, the Mountains and Rivers Order, or Dharma Communications, visit our website at www.mro.org.